Experiencing God

Youth Edition
Leader's Guide

Claude V. King

LifeWay Press
Nashville, Tennessee

ISBN 0-8054-9924-5

Dewey Decimal Classification: 231.5
Subject Heading: GOD—WILL

Unless otherwise indicated, biblical quotations are from:
The Holy Bible, New International Version.
Copyright © 1973, 1978, 1984 by International Bible Society.
Used by permission.

We believe the Bible has God for its author, salvation for its end,
and truth without any mixture of error, for its matter.
The 1963 statement of *The Baptist Faith and Message* is our doctrinal guideline.

Printed in the United States of America
Available from Baptist Book Stores

Produced by the Youth Section
Discipleship and Family Development Division
of The Sunday School Board
of the Southern Baptist Convention
127 Ninth Avenue, North, Nashville, TN 37234

The Writer

Claude V. King is Mission Service Corps Consultant, Office of Prayer and Spiritual Awakening, Home Mission Board of the Southern Baptist Convention. He is active in discipleship training and is becoming recognized as a writer of interactive learning activities. Claude coauthored another LIFE course with John Drakeford entitled *WiseCounsel: Skills for Lay Counseling.* He has served as a volunteer church planter for the Concord Baptist Association of Middle Tennessee. A native of Tennessee, he is a graduate of Belmont College and New Orleans Baptist Theological Seminary. He lives in Murfreesboro, Tennessee, with his wife, Reta, and daughters, Julie and Jenny.

Contents

For Leaders
Leading a Small-Group Study of Experiencing God

Note: Page numbers identified in this Leader's Guide will be preceded by "LG." All other page references refer to pages in the member's book.

Checklist for Leaders

❐ Read and study the youth member book, this Leader's Guide, and view videotape for leaders.
❐ Enlist and train leaders.
  ❐ Decide on the number of groups needed. Have one group for every 10 members.
  ❐ Decide when and where the groups will meet.
  ❐ Develop a time schedule.
  ❐ Develop a system for keeping records.
❐ Introduce *Experiencing God* to youth.
  ❐ Enlist participants.
  ❐ Set and collect fees.
  ❐ Order books and video 10 weeks prior to the first session.
❐ Prepare teaching resources.
  ❐ Prepare posters.
  ❐ Provide chalkboard and chalk or paper and markers.
  ❐ Make one copy of pages 33-41, 43-48 in this Leader's Guide for each member.
  ❐ Provide information on "Keeping a Spiritual Journal" (LG p. 7, 34).
  ❐ Select a theme song.
  ❐ Plan to use the *Experiencing God Youth Video Series* (Item 7700-48).

1. Overview of *Experiencing God, Youth Edition*

Experiencing God is not just a book for reading. It is part of a learning system that is designed to teach the content material and help youth move into a deeper relationship with God. In order to achieve this goal, every element of the learning system should be utilized. Learners need to complete the self-study of their textbook during the week (see p. 5 in member's book). Then learners need to meet in a small group (8 to 10 youth maximum) to review, discuss questions that arise, share personal experiences and insights, and determine ways to apply truths to life.

Experiencing God and other DiscipleLife courses are offered through the Discipleship Training program of a church. If your church does not have a regular training program, you can still offer the course. Some churches are using DiscipleLife courses to start or revitalize their training of disciples through Discipleship Training. If you would like to learn more about DiscipleLife courses, write to DiscipleLife, 127 Ninth Avenue, North, Nashville, TN 37234-0152.

2. Leadership Training and Session Preparation

Watch *Experiencing God Youth Video Series*
Prior to leading the introductory session view the 45 minute *VHS Tape 1 for Leaders*. This message was prepared especially for you. It provides additional insights about how you can best prepare yourself spiritually and practically for this course. Complete the Video Viewing Worksheet for Leader Preparation (LG p. 42) as you watch the video.

How to Use This Guide
This Leader's Guide is designed to help you prepare for and conduct the small-group sessions each week. Much of the preparation for weekly sessions can be completed at one time prior to starting the course. LG pages 33-48 contain materials that are designed for your use in the sessions. You will be given instructions about reproducing copies of these pages for use in your group. Since some of the material is optional, you can use your own judgment about whether you want to provide copies for your group.

LG pages 10-33 provide step-by-step procedures for conducting an introductory session and 9 group sessions. Each group-session plan includes three parts:

• *Before the Session*—This section includes actions for you to complete prior to the group session. Boxes (❐) are provided for you to check as you complete each action. Sessions require a minimum of leader preparation. Take time for prayer and personal spiritual preparation. If you adapt the lesson plans or create activities of your own, you will need to secure resources required for these activities.

• *During the Session*—This section provides learning activities for you to use in conducting a two-hour group session. The activities follow a similar pattern each week.
  The first hour focuses on review of the unit con-

tent, a sharing of personal experiences and responses to that content, and a time to pray for concerns related to the sharing. An optional singing time also is suggested.

The second hour focuses on the use of *Experiencing God Youth Video Series*. After viewing the videotaped message from Henry Blackaby, you will guide your group to discuss and respond to God's message for group members and for your church. By using *all* the elements of this learning system, you will assist youth in developing a deep, fruitful, and confident love relationship with God. (See the large-group/small-group options discussed in this Guide.)

• *After the Session*—This section guides you in evaluating the group session, your performance as a leader, and the needs of youth to help you constantly improve your abilities to guide the group in learning. Each week you are encouraged to think about your group members and identify one or more who may need a personal contact from you.

Before Every Session
Located on page 10 of this Guide is a list of actions that should be taken before every session. As you prepare for each session turn to page 10 and apply each of these steps to the session you are leading. You are reminded of these additional actions each session under "Before the Session."

3. Leadership Enlistment

Your Role as a Small-group Leader
You may be asking yourself, "Why did I agree to teach this class? I need to learn how to know and do God's will myself." Your role in a small-group study is not that of a teacher. You are a leader of learning activities. You are a facilitator of the group-learning process. If you sense God has led you to accept this assignment, you can trust Him to equip and enable you to accomplish the task. As you will learn, you are an instrument through which God wants to do His work. Depend on Him and "pray without ceasing."

Group members will be spending two to three hours or more each unit studying *Experiencing God*. The Holy Spirit is going to be their Teacher. The content and learning activities will help members learn the basic truths and principles during the week. Your job is to help them review what they have learned; share with one another what God has revealed of Himself, His purposes, and His ways; and apply these truths to their personal lives, their family relationships, their school activities, their work, and to your church's life.

Enlist Leaders
Each group will need a separate leader. Your minister of youth or other designated youth leader may want to lead the first group and train others to provide leadership for future groups. If your minister of youth is unable to lead this first group, enlist another of your church's spiritual leaders to guide the group.

Pray that God will help you identify those persons that He wants to lead the groups. These leaders should be spiritually growing Christians and active church members. They should relate well to youth, have a commitment to keep confidential information private, and be willing to spend the time necessary to prepare for the sessions. Look for people who possess skills for leading small-group learning experiences.

4. Organizing and Scheduling Experiencing God Youth Groups

Decide on the Number of Groups Needed
Work with the youth minister, Discipleship Training director, or others to determine how many youth in your church want to study this course at this time. Any youth who has already trusted Jesus Christ as Lord and Savior will benefit from this study. Survey your youth group to determine the number of youth interested in the study. As mentioned earlier, you will need one group for every 10 members. You may want to introduce *Experiencing God* to your youth by conducting a four-session study, retreat, or DiscipleNow using *Lift High the Torch: An Invitation to Experiencing God* (Item 7200-51).

Size of Groups for Effective Learning
Jesus preached to large crowds, but He did most of His discipleship training with a group of 12. He was even closer to three of His disciples who would be key leaders in the New Testament church. You need to provide a learning environment in which group members can ask questions, share personal experiences, and pray intimately with brothers and sisters in Christ. They do not need to be in a crowd where they will be more of a spectator than a participant. Provide a small group for each 10 participants. If you have more than 10 persons interested in participating, provide for multiple groups in order to create the best possible learning environment.

In "During the Session," each activity has a recommended grouping for the activity (entire group, groups of three or four, or pairs). You may decide to use different groupings within your small group. If you do make a change, however, evaluate what members will be sharing, how much time you have, and what size of group would provide for maximum participation by members.

Decide When and Where the Groups Will Meet
The recommended plans for this course call for two-hour sessions each week. Groups should plan to allow for two hours if at all possible. Groups may meet at the church, in homes, or other locations convenient to members. You may want to offer group studies at a variety of times and locations so more youth will be able to participate.

Develop a Time Schedule
A typical two-hour session is divided like this:
First Hour:
   Arrival Activity—5 minutes
   Unit Review—15 minutes
   Sharing Time—25 minutes
   Prayer Time—10 minutes
   Singing/Special Music—5 minutes

Second Hour:
   Break—10 minutes
   Video Viewing—15 minutes
   Video Discussion/Response—30 minutes
   Closure—5 minutes

If you have only one hour per week for your group sessions, select one of these options:

- *Recommended choice:* Take two weeks per unit of study. Complete individual study and use the first hour's agenda for the first group session. Encourage individual review of the unit during the second week and use the second hour's agenda for the second group session. This option would require a minimum of 19 weeks—an introductory session and 18 group sessions.
- *Second choice:* Complete the first-hour agenda during your regular group session and complete the second-hour agenda at another time later in the week. For instance: Use the first-hour agenda during a week night group session. Then offer the second hour's agenda using the videotapes on another night before your weekly youth activities.

Develop a System for Keeping Records
Work with the Discipleship Training director or general secretary to determine the best way of keeping enrollment and attendance records. Participation in a DiscipleLife course such as *Experiencing God* counts toward Discipleship Training participation regardless of the time of week it is offered. Report your weekly attendance to the Discipleship Training director or secretary. If your church does not have an ongoing Discipleship Training program, count participation in *Experiencing God* on the Discipleship Training section of the Annual Uniform Church Letter.

Another reason to keep track of participation involves the Church Study Course. Those persons who complete the individual study of *Experiencing God* and attend the group sessions qualify for the *Experiencing God, Youth Edition,* diploma. These diplomas recognize the significant work of the participant.

5. Introducing Experiencing God to Youth

Enlist Participants
Conduct a retreat or four-session study using *Lift High the Torch: An Invitation to Experiencing God* (Item 7200-51). The closing session provides an opportunity for youth to make a commitment to participate in an *Experiencing God* group. If you do not have enough groups (maximum of 10 per group) to accommodate all those who want to participate, enlist additional leaders. Some leaders may even be willing to lead a second group at a different time during the week.

Invite prospective participants to the introductory session (LG p. 10) through personal contacts, announcements in Sunday School and Discipleship Training, and information in your church newsletter or bulletin. At the end of the session, give those present an opportunity to sign up for the course. If persons are unwilling to make the necessary commitment to the individual and group study, suggest that they not participate at this time. Set a date for the first session, distribute member's books, and make assignments for the first unit.

Two Approaches for Introducing the Study
  •Using *Lift High the Torch*
Leading youth through a study of *Lift High the Torch: An Invitation to Experiencing God* prior to the introductory session will introduce youth to important concepts and principles that they will build on during their nine unit study of *Experiencing God: Knowing and Doing the Will of God, Youth Edition.* Plan and conduct a retreat or four-session study using *Lift High the Torch.* Plan your study at a time when most of your youth can participate. Promote it as a youth-wide event. The final session gives youth an opportunity to make a commitment to be a part of an *Experiencing God* group. One of the best ways to introduce *Experiencing God* to youth is to conduct a DiscipleNow using *Lift High the Torch* during the group sessions. Complete information for planning, promoting, and conducting a DiscipleNow can be found in *DiscipleNow Manual* (Item 7255-78). Leader

helps and guidance material for four complete sessions are included in *Lift High the Torch.*

•Leading Youth Through Introductory Session
The introductory session of *Experiencing God* is still important to prepare youth for the *Experiencing God* study. The first half of the introductory session is for all youth in the youth group. At the conclusion of the first hour they will be given the opportunity to make a commitment to an *Experiencing God* study. Some may have already made the decision to join an *Experiencing God* group during a *Lift High the Torch* study. They will simply indicate their decision. But this session will also allow youth who have not attended a *Lift High the Torch* study, or have prayerfully reconsidered their decision, an opportunity to make a commitment to study *Experiencing God.* The second hour of the introductory session is only for those youth who made a decision to join a group. Be certain to affirm those youth who have made a decision not to join an *Experiencing God* group at this time.

6. Ordering and Providing Resources

Set and Collect Fees
Participants should be expected to pay for the cost of materials. Your church may want to share the cost. Ask participants to pay at least part of the cost. Announce the fee at the times you enlist participants so they will not be embarrassed or surprised at the introductory session. You may want to provide "full scholarships" for those who are unable to participate due to financial reasons.

Provide Spiritual Journals
Participants will need to keep a spiritual journal during the course. This journal will be organized during the introductory session (see LG pp. 10-12) or at least by the first group session. Decide whether you will provide the same kind of notebook for each person and include the cost in the fee for materials or whether you will ask each youth to secure his or her own notebook. Fifty pages should be adequate. Here are several suggestions:
- Three-ring binder with notebook paper and tab dividers. If members select this option, you may suggest that they get a binder large enough to hold their member's book, too.
- Spiral bound notebook, preferably with section dividers included.
- Bound "diary" type book with blank pages.

When you distribute the notebooks, give group members a copy of the instructions on LG page 34—"Keeping a Spiritual Journal."

Plan to provide youth with a copy of *DiscipleHelps: A Daily Quiet Time Guide and Journal* (Item 7217-45) at the completion of the course. This will encourage them to continue keeping a spiritual journal.

Order Resources
Resources should be ordered for the course 8 to 10 weeks prior to the first session. You can estimate the quantity needed by ordering 10 member's books and one leader's guide for each small group. To order see bottom of LG page 47. Resources include:
- *Experiencing God: Knowing and Doing the Will of God, Youth Edition* (Item 7200-08) for members
- *Experiencing God Leader's Guide, Youth Edition* (Item 7200-07) for leaders
- *Experiencing God Youth Video Series* (Item 7700-48)

7. Prepare Teaching Aids

Prepare or Secure Additional Resources
Much of your course preparation can be completed at one time. If you will complete the following actions, you will save time during the course for personal and spiritual preparation.

1. Make one copy of pages 33-41, 43-48, in this Leaders Guide for each member. Some are optional or may be prepared on a poster or chalkboard—use your own judgment. The easiest way is to make photocopies. If possible, use heavier card stock for the Scripture Memory Cards or paste them on card stock after copying. You have permission to copy the following pages, but only for use with *Experiencing God: Knowing and Doing the Will of God, Youth Edition.*

- Keeping a Spiritual Journal instructions (LG p. 34)
- Unit Review Quizzes (LG pp. 36-39) Enlarge to 8½ x 11
- Scripture Memory Cards (LG p. 35)
- *Experiencing God* Course Evaluation (LG p. 40)
- Scriptures for Meditation (LG p. 33)
- Viewing Worksheets for use with each videotape session (LG pp. 43-47).
- Church Study Course Enrollment/Credit Request Form 725 (p. 160, LG p. 48). Making copies of this form will keep members from having to cut the form out of their books.

2. Prepare the following posters:
- Memorizing Scripture poster—Turn to "Help Members Memorize Scripture" (LG p. 8). Write the boldface instructions or key words on a poster for use in the introductory and small-group sessions.
- Seven Realities poster—On poster board draw a

copy of the diagram that appears on the inside back cover of the member's book. Using a different color of marker, write the key words for each of the seven realities on the diagram. Since you will use this poster throughout the course, you will need to protect it.

- Two diagram posters described (LG p. 22)—Prepare and enlarge to 8½ x 11.
- Unit posters—Enlist group members to help prepare posters for use with each unit. Read through the summary statements at the end of each day's lesson. Select three to five statements or Scriptures from each unit that seem to best capture the meaning of the unit for you. Hand print the statements on construction paper or 1/4 sheets of poster board. On the back of each poster write the unit number for use later. You may want to laminate or spray them with clear plastic to protect them for repeated use.

3. If you plan to display copies of other DiscipleLife courses or Discipleship Training resources for youth in session 9, order them now. Before ordering, check with your church media library or appropriate leader to see if your church already has copies that can be used for the display.

4. Provide chalkboard and chalk or newsprint and a marker for use throughout the course. Extra sheets of paper will be required in several sessions. Keep a supply of paper and pencils in your room.

Select a Theme Song

People learn much of their theology through songs or hymns. Music is also a valuable way to stimulate an affective (spiritual/emotional) response to the topics being studied. Consider selecting and singing (or playing a recorded version) of a theme song for this study. You might consider a hymn like "He's Everything to Me" or a contemporary chorus.

Help Members Memorize Scripture

You will cut apart and hand out the Scripture Memory Cards each week. Some youth may not be skilled at memorizing Scripture. The following suggestions may be helpful. Write the boldface instructions on a poster for use in the introductory and first small-group session. Explain each suggestion.

1. **Seek understanding.** Read the verse in its context. For instance, for John 15:5 you might read John 15:1-17. Study the verse and try to understand what it means.
2. **Read the verse aloud several times.**
3. **Write the verse and reference several times on a** separate sheet of paper. Refer to the Scripture Memory card as often as needed for accuracy.
4. **Quote the verse one phrase at a time.** Divide the verse into short and meaningful phrases. Quote the first phrase word-for-word. Then build on it by learning the second phrase. Continue until you are able to quote the entire verse word-for-word.
5. **Repeat the verse to another person** and ask him to check your accuracy.
6. **Review the memorized verse regularly.** During the first week, carry the card in your pocket or purse. Review it several times daily during waiting periods—like riding an elevator, riding to school or work, during lunch. Review the verse at least daily for the first six weeks. Review weekly for the next six weeks and monthly thereafter.

8. Using Experiencing God Youth Video Series

Large-group Video Viewing

Many churches may have more than one small group studying *Experiencing God, Youth Edition*, at one time. In this case you may want to schedule a large-group time for the video viewing. Your minister of youth or other assigned leader can guide the video-viewing time. In a large-group setting provide a separate video monitor for each 25 participants.

If it is necessary to use this large-group option for video viewing, be sure to provide small-group sharing times for effective learning and participation to take place. Small groups should remain the same throughout the course.

Plan to Use the Videotapes

The *Experiencing God Youth Video Series* feature Henry Blackaby in a youth setting teaching throughout each of the units. The videotapes feature Henry in dialog with youth and answering their questions. The videotapes provide inspiring illustrations, additional explanation, and answers to questions related to the corresponding unit. The messages that will be used in this youth edition are:

- an overview for introducing the course
- a message on preparation for the course leader
- nine 10-minute segments (one for use with each unit)

These videotapes are recommended for this DiscipleLife course and are included in the group session plans. The cost of the videotapes becomes an ongoing investment in the life of your church as group after group benefits from Henry's teaching.

Because the tapes were designed for *supplementary use* with the printed book, they were never intended to stand alone as a conference. They are interrelated to the printed resources. Persons who only watch the videotapes will miss many of the basic truths, biblical texts, and especially the learning experiences through which God works to encounter them in real and personal ways. Some of the videotaped segments may be used to stimulate interest and enlist participation in a small-group study of the complete course.

Using the Video Viewing Worksheets
Included in this Leader's Guide are nine reproducible Video Viewing Worksheets (LG p. 43-47). These worksheets have been designed for use while viewing each video segment. The Video Viewing Worksheets begin with Unit 1. Encourage youth to take notes on these worksheets.

9. Responding to Group Concerns

Answering Difficult Questions
Group members will ask some questions that you cannot answer. Expect them. Welcome them. Apply what you are learning. When you do not have the answer (or maybe even when you do), encourage the group to join you in praying and searching the Scriptures. Together, ask God to guide you to His answer, to His viewpoint or perspective. Then trust Him to provide the answer. When God sends the answer through one or more group members, you all will know more of God and His ways because of the experience.

Responding to God's Activity in a Group
One of the lessons you need to learn from the Lord is how to respond to God's activity in a group experience. We have not been taught how to respond when God interrupts our group activities, plans, or programs. This is a lesson God can and will teach you. You can depend on Him. He cares far more for your group than you do. If He wants to work in the midst of that group to reveal Himself, He can and will enable you to respond appropriately. You must make some prior commitments in the way you function as a spiritual leader. You must give your plans and agenda to God. If God interrupts your group, cancel your agenda and see what He wants to do.

Here are some suggestions for responding to God's activity in your group.
- Place your absolute trust in God to guide you when He wants to work in your group setting.
- Decide beforehand that you will cancel your agenda and give God freedom to move anytime He

shows you that He wants to do a special work. As you will learn during this study, there are some things only God can do. When you see Him at work in your group, that is your invitation to join Him.
- Watch for things like tears of joy or conviction, emotional or spiritual brokenness, the thrill of a new insight, or a need for prayer in response to a need. These things are sometimes seen only as a facial expression. Determine whether you need to talk to the person now with the group or privately. You must depend on the Holy Spirit for such guidance.
- Respond by asking a probing question like one of these: Is something happening in your life that you would share with us? How can we pray for you? Would you share with us what God is doing in your life? What can we do to be of help to you?
- If the person responds by sharing, then provide ministry based on the need. If he or she does not seem ready to respond, do not push or pressure. Give God time to work in the person's life.
- Invite group members to minister to one another. This may be to pray, to comfort, to counsel privately, or to rejoice with the person. When you do not feel equipped to deal with a problem that surfaces, ask the group if one of them feels led to help. You will be amazed at how God works to provide just the right person to provide the needed ministry.
- Give youth the opportunity to testify to what God is doing. This is a very critical point. Often the testimony of one person may be used of God to help another person with an identical problem or challenge. This is also one of the best ways for youth to experience God by hearing testimony of His wonderful work in the life of another person. Do not hide God's glory from His people.
- When you do not sense a clear direction about what to do next, ask the group. Or, you may want to say, "I do not have a clear sense of what we need to do next. Does anyone have a sense of what God would want us to do?"

If God wants to work in the midst of a group, He can and will give the guidance needed for that time. Your job is to learn to know His voice and then do everything you sense He wants you to do. At the same time, trust Him to work through His body—the church. He has placed members in your group and gifted them to build up the body of Christ. Acknowledge and use all of the resources God has given to your group.

Start Here

Introducing Experiencing God

Session Goals: This session will help potential members (1) understand the approach of the study and how it will help them move into a deeper relationship with God; (2) realize the commitments required for studying this DiscipleLife course; and (3) demonstrate a commitment to complete the personal study and group session requirements for this course.

AGENDA

1. Arrival Activity (10 Min.)
2. Course Overview (30)
3. Life Commitments (10)
4. Decision Time (5)
5. Singing/Special Music (5)
6. Break (10)
7. Getting Ready for Next Week (35)
8. Covenant Making (10)
9. Closure (5)

BEFORE EVERY SESSION

❑ Prepare yourself spiritually for the upcoming study. Ask God to draw youth to the introductory session that He wants to involve in this study.

❑ Read through "During the Session." Adapt or develop the activities in a way that will help the youth understand the overview of the content and will guide them in making a commitment to participate.

❑ Note the time suggested for each activity. Adjust as necessary. Write a time in the margin to indicate when each activity should begin (for instance, 6:15 beside "Unit Review").

❑ If you already have prepared the unit posters (LG p. 7), display one from each unit on a focal wall to create interest.

❑ Optional: Select a hymn, chorus, or recorded song for use during the group time. Arrange for someone to play the piano, or bring a tape or CD player.

❑ Read through the descriptions of the learning activities in "During the Session" and identify the sections of content in the member's book that you will be explaining and discussing in the session. Study those sections of material. If you want help, enlist persons to explain various sections.

❑ Enlist someone to provide refreshments for break.

BEFORE THE SESSION

❑ Secure the following items and include others that you need for activities you may have developed on your own.
* Individual copies of worksheets 1 and 2 for each group member (LG p. 41).
* Seven Realities poster (LG p. 41).
* Poster with names of God from pages 157-158. (Select at least one name of God by which you know Him because of experience.)
* Memorizing Scripture poster (LG p. 8).
* Copies of a sign-up sheet with a line for the name and the four choices listed in point 4 of "During the Session" ("Decision Time").

❑ If you are using the videotape overview, do the following:
* Secure and set up the equipment necessary for viewing.
* Preview the "Course Overview" segment of the videotape. List one or two key ideas or questions that you think will be of interest to your youth. Use these ideas to introduce the videotape.

❑ If you have not completed all the preparations in "Leading a Small-group Study of *Experiencing God*" (LG pp. 4-9), do so before the introductory session.

DURING THE SESSION

1. Arrival Activity
* **Greet prospective members as they arrive**. Give each person a copy of worksheet 1. Ask them to complete the activity while others are coming in.

* **Lead in an opening prayer.** Pray that God will use this session to give insight into His ways of revealing His will to people and that He will guide each person present to respond to Him in making a decision about whether to study *Experiencing God, Youth Edition*.

2. Course Overview
* **Review worksheet 1.** Briefly review answers to the questions in the learning activity on "Worksheet 1: Jesus' Example."
* **Explain seven realities.** Distribute worksheet 2.

Ask the youth to read the seven statements and circle a key word or phrase in each one. Using the explanation and Scriptures on pages 18-21 as background and the Seven Realities poster, briefly explain how Moses' experience with God is an example of this pattern of God's working through people.

• **Experiencing God.** Display the poster of some names of God. Explain how we come to know God by experience (p. 55). Describe Abraham's experience in Genesis 22:1-18 (pp. 55-56) as an example of how a person comes to know God by experience. Give a personal example. Then ask for a volunteer or two to briefly describe an experience in which he or she came to know God by one of the names on the poster.

• **Course explanation.** Choose one of the following depending upon whether you have videotapes.
   a. *Videotapes.* Show the three-minute "Course Overview" segment for this session.
   b. *Live.* Share with the group your reasons for leading this course. Then read the list of unit titles on the contents page (p. 3). Explain that this is not just a course. And it is not a method or seven easy steps to knowing God's will. The course is designed to help members into a relationship in which they clearly hear when God is speaking, realize where God is working, join Him in His work, and experience Him working through them to accomplish His purposes.

3. Life Commitments

• **Explain requirements.** Use the introduction (p. 5) to explain requirements of self-study and participation in small-group sessions. Emphasize that participants will need to spend about 30 minutes per day for five days each week in completing assignments.

• **Read Covenant.** Read the Experiencing God Group Covenant (p. 159) that members will be asked to sign if they decide to participate.

• **Announce schedule.** Announce time and place when groups will be meeting to study *Experiencing God, Youth Edition.*

• **Questions and answers.** Allow time for youth to ask questions about the course.

4. Decision Time

• **Pray.** Ask youth to pray silently about what God wants them to do regarding this study. Close the prayer time, asking God to clearly guide all the persons present.

• **Sign-up time.** Pass around the sign-up sheets that you prepared. Direct each youth to write their name on the sheet and indicate one of the following: (1) Enroll me for the current study. (2) Notify me about the next time the course is offered. (3) Please consider offering this study at another time (please specify day and time). (4) I'm unable to participate at this time.

5. Singing/Special Music

• **Optional special music.** While youth are signing the sheets, sing familiar hymns or choruses or play a recorded song that relates to one of the subjects of this study. If you have selected a theme song for the study, sing it now.

6. Break

• **Provide refreshments.** Explain that, in the following hour, you will be distributing materials and giving specific instructions to those who plan to participate in the upcoming study. Invite everyone to enjoy the refreshments.

7. Getting Ready for Next Week

• **Distribute materials.** Give each person the following materials:
   a. *Experiencing God: Knowing and Doing the Will of God, Youth Edition.*
   b. Spiritual journey notebook or instructions (LG p. 34).
   c. Copy of the Scripture Memory Cards (LG p. 35) and the Scriptures for Meditation (LG p. 33).

• **Explain self-study requirements.** Using Unit 1 as an example, walk the members through the process they will follow in completing each unit of study. Here are some suggestions for this overview:
   a. Point out the verse of Scripture to memorize on page 6. Use the Memorizing Scripture poster you prepared to give suggestions for memorizing Scripture. Call attention to the Scripture Memory Cards you gave members. Explain that they can cut the cards apart and keep them in a pocket or purse for regular review.
   b. Mention the introduction (p. 5) and ask them to review the information as they begin the study.
   c. Explain how the content is divided into five assignments. Encourage members to study only one day at a time, so that they will have time to cultivate an intimacy with God on a daily basis.
   d. Explain the interaction between the content and the learning activities that are indicated by a burning-bush symbol and boldface type. For an example, ask members to turn to page 9 and complete the first multiple choice question.
   e. Explain that the first two units give an overview of the way God works with and in the lives of people. Units 3-9 go into greater detail on each of the seven realities of experiencing God.
   f. Ask members to turn to page 10 and notice the end-of-the-day review. Mention that this daily activity is designed for them to listen to what God may want to say to them. Mention that they

may want to keep a running summary in their spiritual journal.

• **Explain Spiritual Journal.** Distribute copies of the "Keeping a Spiritual Journal" instructions (LG p. 34). Point out the kinds of information they will want to record in their journals and how they may want to divide the notebook into categories. Ask members to bring their journals, Bible, and workbooks to each group session, because they will be used each week.

8. Covenant Making

• **Prepare the covenant.** Ask members to turn to page 159. Read again the covenant agreements. Give members an opportunity to discuss any changes or additions they want to make. Seek full agreement on the covenant. Then ask members to make the changes agreed to on their copies. Ask them to fill in their name at the top.

• **Pray about keeping the covenant.** Join hands and pray that God will draw this group into a deeper fellowship with Him and with one another during the coming weeks. Ask each person to pray a one-sentence prayer asking for God's strength and guidance to complete the course and keep this covenant.

• **Sign the covenant.** Ask individuals to sign their own covenant and then sign the covenant of other group members.

9. Closure

• **Lead in a prayer of commitment.** Express your feelings about studying together with this group. Be sure to affirm those who have decided not to participate at this time. Then ask one of the members to lead the group in a prayer of commitment to God and to one another for the duration of this course.

1. Add to your spiritual journal the names of group members and ways you can pray for each person. Do you sense a need to pray intently for any one person in particular? If so, record concerns you need to pray about for that person.

2. Ask yourself the following questions and jot notes in your spiritual journal or on a separate paper.
   • What spiritual or mental preparation do I need to make for the next session that may have been lacking this week?
   • How well did I do at beginning and ending on time?

3. Save all posters for use in later sessions or for a future introductory session.

4. Give information from the sign-up sheets to the appropriate person in your church. Encourage your Discipleship Training director to make every possible effort to provide a group study for those who request a time different from the one selected for your group.

5. If you had more than 10 youth in your group, enlist an additional leader and divide the group prior to the next session.

6. If you do not have enough member's books, check with your local Baptist Book Store or LifeWay Christian Book Store for copies or call 1-800-458-BSSB and place an order. A customer service representative will help you get the materials as quickly as possible.

Session

1

God's Will and Your Life

Session Goals: This session will help potential members (1) understand the approach of the study and how it will help them move into a deeper relationship with God; (2) realize the commitments required for studying this DiscipleLife course; and (3) demonstrate a commitment to complete the personal study and group session requirements for this course.

AGENDA
1. Arrival Activity (15 Min.)
2. Unit Review (20)
3. Sharing Time (10)
4. Praying Time (10)
5. Singing/Special Music (5)
6. Break (10)
7. Video Viewing and Discussion (45)
8. Closure (5)

BEFORE THE SESSION

❏ Refer to **"Before Every Session"** checklist (LG p. 10) for use with this session.

❏ Arrange the chairs in a tight circle.

❏ Prepare seven Scripture-reference slips. Write each of the following Scripture references on a separate slip of paper: John 7:16; John 8:28-29; John 10:37-38; John 12:49-50; John 14:10; John 17:8; Acts 2:22.

❏ Gather the following items and include any others that you need for activities you developed.
  • one copy of Get Acquainted statements (LG p. 36) for each person
  • one copy of Unit 1 Review Quiz (LG p. 36) for each person
  • Memorizing Scripture poster from introductory session
  • Seven Realities poster from introductory session
  • one copy of Viewing Worksheet 1 (LG p. 43) for each person

❏ Prepare a one-minute preview of Unit 2.

❏ If you are using the videotape, do the following:
  • Set up the equipment necessary for viewing.
  • Preview the videotape segment for this session and list one or two key ideas or questions that you think will be of special interest to your group. Use these ideas to introduce the videotape.
  • Think through your own response to the video discussion question in point 7 of "During the Session" ("Video Viewing and Discussion").
  • Prepare to lead youth in a brief discussion using the Viewing Worksheet.

Note: Each time you divide the group into pairs or groups of three or four, give verbal instructions to everyone. If you think they need additional help, write the instructions on a chalkboard or newsprint.

DURING THE SESSION

1. Arrival Activity

• **Greet members as they arrive.** Use this first activity together as a get-acquainted time. Give each youth a copy of the "Get Acquainted" statements that follow. While others are coming in, ask members to complete the statements on a separate sheet of paper.
  a. My name is . . .
  b. The thing I like best about my hometown is . . .
  c. I accepted Jesus Christ as my Lord and Savior when . . .
  d. Something interesting you might not know about me is . . .
  e. I chose to study this course on knowing and doing the will of God because . . .

• **Locate Scripture.** As some finish writing, give to different members the seven Scripture-reference slips you prepared. Ask each one to find the Scripture and mark it for reading later in the session.

• **Get acquainted.** Form groups of three or four. Ask members to share responses to a, b, and c. After this sharing, have them share responses to d and e. Collect the papers so you will have names, addresses, and phone numbers.

• **Opening prayer.** After youth have had time to share, gather the group into a circle. Lead in prayer, thanking God for bringing them together. Acknowledge God's presence in your midst and ask the Holy Spirit to be your Teacher. Ask Him to bond your lives together in Christian love and unity during the study.

2. Unit Review

• **Review quiz.** Distribute copies of the review quiz for Unit 1. Ask youth to complete the quiz. Allow them to check their own papers. Tell youth that they will be asked to complete a quiz like this for each unit. Explain that the quizzes are not tests but are simply for review they will check their own answers.

• **Discuss seven realities.** Display the poster of the seven realities diagram. Mention the key words for the first reality and ask someone to state it in her own words. Do the same for each of the other six realities.

• **Discuss Jesus' example.** Ask one youth to read the summary of Jesus' example for following the will of His Father (p. 12). Then call for the seven Scriptures to be read by the persons enlisted earlier in the session. Suggest they mark these verses in their Bibles or write them in their books on page 12.

Call for volunteers to answer the following questions: (1) Who was doing the work we see in the life of Jesus? Was Jesus doing His own work, or was God the Father doing His work through Jesus? (2) Whose words did Jesus speak, His own or His Father's?

• **Ask volunteers to answer the following questions:**
  a. What are two things a servant must do to be used by God? (p. 14)
  b. Why does God like to do His work through ordinary people? (p. 22 and 1 Cor. 1:26-31)

3. Sharing Time

• **Memorize Scripture.** Form pairs. Ask them to quote John 15:5 to each other. If some have trouble, give words of encouragement and review the suggestions for memorizing Scripture (LG p. 8). Ask the pairs to share with each other what God may have said to them through this week's memory verse.

• **Review meaningful Scripture.** Forms groups of three or four. Ask them to review their five "most meaningful" statements or Scriptures for the unit (pp. 10, 13, 16, 19, and 22) and identify the one statement or Scripture that was most meaningful of these five. Tell them to (a) read their most meaningful statements or Scriptures; (b) state why they were meaningful; and (c) share how they responded to God.

• **Declare the wonderful works of the Lord.** Reassemble the group and allow time for testimonies. Say: If God has done something special in or through your life this past week, please share what He has done so we can praise the Lord together.

• **Focus on God.** Ask: (a) What have you come to know about God, His purposes, or His ways this week? (b) What do you sense God wants you to do in response to Him?

4. Praying Time

• **Share requests and pray.** In the groups of three or four formed earlier, ask each youth to share one way the others can pray for him or her. Suggest that they pray for one member at a time by allowing several to pray for that youth. Ask the group to continue praying until everyone has been prayed for. Tell the groups that a person does not have to pray aloud unless he or she wants to.

• **Record prayer requests.** As groups finish praying, suggest: Turn to the prayer section of your journal and record prayer requests or ways God led you to pray for individuals in your group. Remember these persons in your prayer times next week.

5. Singing/Special Music

•**Optional special music.** Sing a hymn or chorus or play a recorded song that relates to servanthood or following Jesus' example, such as "Footsteps of Jesus" or "Where Ever He Leads I'll Go." If you chose a theme song for your group, practice singing it now.

6. Break

7. Video Viewing and Discussion

• **Introduce the video.** Share one or two key ideas that you think will be of special interest to the youth. Hand out the Viewing Worksheet.

• **View the videotape.** Show the videotape.

• **Discussion.** Form groups of three. Have them discuss the following question and prepare to share a brief report: What adjustments do you need to make to God in your personal life, in your school relationships, in your family, or in your church relationships?

• **Reporting.** Call for reports and guide a brief discussion as time permits using the Worksheet.

• **Prayer response.** Ask a member to offer a prayer response on behalf of individuals and your church.

8. Closure

• **Waiting on the Lord.** Review any questions or concerns that may have come up during the session. Ask the group to pray for these concerns and seek answers during the coming week.

• **Preview Unit 2.** Ask youth to note the difference between self-centered and God-centered living.

• **Pray.** Stand and join hands. Ask each youth to pray a one-sentence prayer of personal commitment to God for the duration of this course. Add that anyone who doesn't want to pray out loud can "pass" by squeezing the hand of the person next to him or her.

AFTER THE SESSION

1. Record in the prayer section of your own spiritual journal specific ways you can pray for group members. Do you sense a need to pray intently for any one youth in particular? Record concerns you need to pray about for that youth.

2. Ask yourself the following questions and jot notes in your spiritual journal or on a separate paper.

• What resources, if any, do I need to get for group members? Does everyone have a member's book and spiritual journal?

• What spiritual or mental preparation do I need to make for the next session that may have been lacking this week?

• Which of the youth need to be encouraged to participate more in the sharing and discussion times? When and how will I encourage them?

• When could I have responded more appropriately to the needs of youth or to the leadership of the Holy Spirit?

• Did I begin and end on time? If not, why?

• Which members most need a phone call this week for encouragement, prayer, instruction, correction, or counsel? When will I make the calls?

3. If you had more than 10 youth, divide it and enlist another leader. If you cannot enlist another leader, consider dividing into two groups and meeting at different times during the week.

4. Read through "Before the Session" on the following page to get an idea of the preparation that will be required for your next group session.

Session

2

Looking to God

Session Goals: This session will help members (1) state in their own words the seven realities of experiencing God; (2) define the difference between self-centered and God-centered living and give one biblical example of each viewpoint; and (3) yield their wills to the lordship of Christ.

AGENDA

1. Arrival Activity (5 Min.)
2. Unit Review (15)
3. Sharing Time (25)
4. Praying Time (10)
5. Singing/Special Music (5)
6. Break (10)
7. Video Viewing and Discussion (45)
8. Closure (5)

BEFORE THE SESSION

❏ Refer to **"Before Every Session"** checklist (LG p. 10) for use with this session.

❏ Gather together the following items and include any others you need for activities that you may have developed on your own:
  • one copy of Unit 2 Review Quiz and Sharing Time topics (LG p. 36) for each person
  • Seven Realities poster
  • one copy of Viewing Worksheet 2 (LG p. 43) for each person

❏ Make sure each member has a member's book and a spiritual journal. If you know of a member who does not have both, try to get them to the member for use before the group session. Be sure any new members have both resources and that they understand the need to complete the learning activities in the unit prior to your group session. After this session, no new members should begin the course.

❏ Remove the unit posters from the previous session and save them for use in a future study of *Experiencing God, Youth Edition*. Display the posters you have prepared for Unit 2 (LG pp. 7-8).

❏ Prepare a one-minute preview of Unit 3.

❏ If you are using the videotape, do the following:
  • Set up the equipment necessary for viewing.
  • Preview the videotape segment for this session and list one or two key ideas or questions that you think will be of special interest to your group. Use these ideas to introduce the videotape.
  • Think through your own response to the video discussion question in point 7 of "During the Session" ("Video Viewing and Discussion").
  • Prepare to lead youth in a brief discussion using the Viewing Worksheet.

DURING THE SESSION

1. Arrival Activity

  • **Greet members as they arrive**. Give each youth a copy of the unit review quiz to work on while others are coming in. Ask them to complete the quiz and then make sure they have completed the learning activities that will be discussed in the "Sharing Time."

  • **Opening prayer.** Ask for a volunteer to open the session with prayer. Suggest that all members pray silently for God to guide them to a more God-centered living.

2. Unit Review

  • **Review quiz.** Review and discuss, if needed, the answers to the review quiz. Remind members that they will have a quiz like this each session to begin a review of the unit's content. Encourage them to complete all the learning activities in each unit prior to the group session, so that they can actively participate in the discussion and sharing times.

  • **Review seven realities.** Using the Seven Realities poster, review the statements of the seven realities of experiencing God. See if members can state (in their own words) the seven realities without hints. If they have trouble, give them the key words.

  • **Ask volunteers to answer the following questions:**
  a. What is the difference between self-centered and God-centered living? (p. 24)
  b. How is King Asa an example of both kinds of living? (p. 25)
  c. How did George Mueller seek God's directions for his life? (pp. 31-32)

d. How did God speak in the Old Testament? During the life of Jesus? (pp. 33-34)

e. How does God speak in our day? (p. 34)

f. What is the key to knowing God's voice? (p. 34)

• **Discuss the poster**. Focus attention on the statements on the unit posters. Read each statement and ask members to comment on what that statement means to them. Ask what adjustments may be needed in their lives to relate correctly to God.

3. Sharing Time

• **Memorize Scripture.** Form pairs. Say, Quote Psalm 20:7 to each other and share what God may have said to you through this week's memory verse.

• **Written responses.** Form groups of three or four. Instruct youth to share their answers on their unit review quiz and then turn in their books to the following learning activities to share and discuss.

a. Statements about God's judgment in the section "You Need to Know What God Is About to Do" (p. 28).

b. The four questions on lordship and character building at the bottom of page 37.

c. One of the most meaningful statements or Scriptures from this unit's lessons and your prayer response to God. Choose one from pages 26, 29, 32, 35, and 38.

• **Focus on God.** Ask: What have you come to know about God, His purposes, or His ways this week? What do you sense God wants you to do in response to this knowledge of Him?

• **Declare the wonderful works of the Lord**. Ask for testimonies. Say: If God has done something special in or through your life this last week, share what He has done, so we can praise the Lord together.

4. Praying Time

• **Record prayer requests**. Ask members to turn to the prayer section of their journals and prepare to record the prayer requests that are shared in the following activity.

• **Share requests and pray**. Ask each person to give the group a one-sentence prayer request. The request could relate to the individual, his or her family, school, church, work, a friend, or a relative. Suggest that some requests may focus on spiritual concerns that have arisen as a result of this study. After each person has shared, ask members to pray conversationally for the needs expressed by others.

5. Singing/Special Music

• **Optional special music**. Sing a hymn or chorus or play a recorded song that relates to God's way or responding to God's initiative. A song such as "Take My Life, Lead Me, Lord" would be suitable.

6. Break

7. Video Viewing and Discussion

• **Introduce the video.** Share one or two key ideas that you think will be of special interest to the youth. Hand out the Viewing Worksheet.

• **View the videotape.** Show the videotape segment for this session.

• **Discussion.** Form groups of three or four. Direct them to discuss the following questions and prepare to share a brief report: Why do we need to wait on the Lord to receive instructions about what He wants to do through us? What are some things we should do or not do in trying to follow God's will? (For instance: Don't dream your own dreams about what you want to do for God.)

• **Reporting.** Call for reports and guide a brief discussion as time permits using the Worksheet.

• **Prayer Response.** Ask one youth to offer a prayer response on behalf of individuals and your church.

8. Closure

• **Waiting on the Lord.** Review any questions or concerns that may have come up during the session. Ask the group to pray for these concerns and seek answers during the coming week.

• **Preview Unit 3.** Preview the unit by asking members to pay special attention to the worship assignment on Day 3 and allot ample time for their "walk with God."

• **Pray.** Stand in a tight circle and join hands. Call on one member to voice a prayer of commitment for the group that they always will look only to God for directions in His kingdom's work.

AFTER THE SESSION

1. Add to your spiritual journal specific ways you can pray for group members. Do you sense a need to pray intently for any one person in particular? If so, record concerns you need to pray about for that person. Include in your journal any concerns for your church that may have surfaced during the session. Pray for these concerns during the coming week.

2. Ask yourself the following questions and jot notes in your spiritual journal or on a separate paper.

• What resources, if any, do I need to get?

• What spiritual or mental preparation do I need to make for the next session that may have been lacking this week?

- Which of the members need to be encouraged to participate more in the sharing and discussion times? When and how will I encourage them?

- When could I have responded more appropriately to the needs of members or to the leadership of the Holy Spirit?

- How well did I do at beginning and ending on time?

- Which members most need a card or note of encouragement this week? When will I write and mail it?

3. Take some time in the next day or two to seek God's evaluation of your group leadership. Are you allowing Him to guide you? Are you trusting Him to do the spiritual things only He can do, or are you trying to pressure response yourself? Do you see God's activity in the lives of the group members?

Now take time to thank God for the privilege of being His servant.

4. Read through "Before the Session" on the following page to get an idea of the preparation that will be required for your next group session.

Session

3

God Pursues a Love Relationship

Session Goals: This session will help members (1) quote the first two statements of the realities of experiencing God; (2) identify biblical examples in which a love relationship with God is real, personal, and practical; and (3) identify and verbalize times in their own lives when they experienced God as real, personal, and practical.

AGENDA

1. Arrival Activity (5 Min.)
2. Unit Review (15)
3. Sharing Time (25)
4. Praying Time (10)
5. Singing/Special Music (5)
6. Break (10)
7. Video Viewing and Discussion (45)
8. Closure (5)

BEFORE THE SESSION

❏ Refer to **"Before Every Session"** checklist (LG p. 10) for use with this session.
❏ Gather together the following items and include any others you need for activities that you may have developed on your own:

- one copy of Unit 3 Review Quiz and Sharing Time topics (LG p. 36) for each person
- Seven Realities poster
- one copy of Viewing Worksheet 3 (LG. p. 44) for each person
❏ Prepare a one-minute preview of Unit 4.
❏ If you are using the videotape, do the following:
  - Set up the equipment necessary for viewing.
  - Preview the videotape segment for this session and list one or two key ideas or questions that you think will be of special interest to your group. Use these ideas to introduce the videotape.
  - Think through your own response to the video discussion question in point 7 of "During the Session" ("Video Viewing and Discussion").
  - Prepare to lead youth in a brief discussion using the Viewing Worksheet.

DURING THE SESSION

1. Arrival Activity
- **Greet members as they arrive**. Give each youth a copy of the unit review quiz to work on while others are coming in. Ask them to complete the quiz and to make sure they have completed the learning activities that will be discussed in the "Sharing Time."
- **Opening prayer.** Ask members to voice statements of praise, thanksgiving, and adoration to God for who He is and what He has done. Close with a prayer, asking for God's guidance for the session.

2. Unit Review

• **Review quiz.** Discuss the answers to questions A and B on the review quiz. Ask questions like these:

  a. What are you becoming in Christ?

  b. How should that influence your life today?

  c. How did Paul deal with his past?

  d. Can a person take the initiative in establishing a love relationship with God? Why or why not? (No. Whenever a person seeks after God, he does so because God is drawing him. See Day 4, p. 48.)

• **Review seven realities.** Form pairs. Ask them to state to each other the first two realities of experiencing God. If they need hints, give them the key words *God's work* and *relationship.*

• **Ask volunteers to answer the following questions:**

  a. What are some ways God has demonstrated His love for us? (p. 42)

  b. How can we show our love for God? (p. 42)

  c. What are some biblical examples in which a relationship with God was real, personal, and practical? (pp. 51-52)

• **Poster discussion.** Focus attention on the statements on the unit posters you have displayed. One-by-one, read the statements and ask members to comment on what each statement means to them. Ask what adjustments may be needed in their lives to relate correctly to God.

3. Sharing Time

• **Scripture memory.** Form pairs. Ask members to quote Matthew 22:37-38 to each other and share what God may have said to them through this memory selection.

• **Written responses.** Form groups of three or four. Ask members to turn in their books to the following learning activities and share responses with one another. Topics are listed in the "Sharing Time" box with the review quiz.

  a. Things in which you are investing your life, time, and resources and the adjustments God wants you to make (p. 45).

  b. Reasons you know God loves you (p. 48).

  c. An experience when God was real, personal, or practical in His relationship to you (p. 52).

  d. One of the most meaningful statements or Scriptures from this unit's lessons and your prayer response to God. Choose one from pages 42, 45, 50, or 53.

  e. Answers to these questions: What have you come to know about God, His purposes, or His ways this week? What do you sense God wants you to do in response to this knowledge of Him?

• **Walk with God.** Reassemble the group and ask volunteers to share their feelings about their "walking with God" experience recorded at the end of Day 3 (p. 47). Share your own experience as a model for others.

• **Declare the wonderful works of the Lord.** Allow time for testimonies. Say: If God has done something special in or through your life this last week, please share what God has done, so we can praise the Lord together.

4. Praying Time

• **Pray Psalm 103.** Ask members to turn in their Bibles to Psalm 103. As an expression of gratitude to God for His love, join in a group reading of this Psalm. Remind members that blessing the Lord through this reading can be a form of worship and prayer. Suggest that one member read a verse, then the person to her left read the second verse. Continue reading one verse at a time until you have completed reading the entire Psalm.

• **Expressing your love to God.** Form groups of three or four. Ask them to spend the remaining few minutes expressing their love to God in prayer. This may include thanksgiving, praise, or statements of commitment.

5. Singing/Special Music

• **Optional special music.** Sing a hymn or chorus or play a recorded song that relates to love for God and God's love for you. You might select a song like "Jesus Paid It All"; "In the Garden"; "Love Lifted Me"; or "More than Wonderful." If time permits, ask for any special requests and sing one or two.

6. Break

7. Video Viewing and Discussion

• **Introduce the video.** Share one or two key ideas that you think will be of special interest to the youth. Hand out the Viewing Worksheet.

• **View the videotape.** Show the videotape segment for this session.

• **Discussion.** Ask, What is the most meaningful thing you heard on this portion of the videotape and why? What do you sense you need to do in response to God after hearing the message in this videotape?

• **Reporting.** Call for reports and guide a brief discussion as time permits using the Worksheet.

• **Prayer response.** Ask members to kneel at their chairs and spend a few minutes responding to God privately. Suggest that they may want to ask God for forgiveness, healing of emotional scars of the past, or for help in dealing with some other issue that God brings to mind.

• **Testimonies.** Give members an opportunity to

share what God may have been doing in their lives during this week and during this session. Do not, however, force youth to share if they do not feel impressed to do so. As a leader, you need to be very sensitive to what may be happening during this time. If God reveals to you that He is moving deeply in a person's life, this is a time to "make major adjustments." If one or more individuals are deeply moved by this time of prayer and testimony, you need to spend some extra time with the ones deeply touched by the Lord. Enlist the help of other group members to pray with and for these individuals. Stay with them until they experience a sense a peace about this encounter with God.

8. Closure
• **Waiting on the Lord.** Review any questions or concerns that may have come up during the session. Ask the group to pray for these concerns and seek answers during the coming week.
• **Preview Unit 4.** Preview Unit 4 by asking youth to pay special attention to how God reveals His invitation for them to join Him in His work.
• **Pray.** Form groups of three or four. Ask them to close the session by thanking God and praying for the other three members in their group. Suggest that members leave quietly as the others finish praying.

AFTER THE SESSION

---

1. Add to your spiritual journal specific ways you can pray for group members. Do you sense a need to pray intently for any one person in particular? If so, record concerns you need to pray about for that person.

2. Ask yourself the following questions and jot notes in your spiritual journal or on a separate paper.

• What spiritual or mental preparation do I need to make for the next session that may have been lacking this week?

• Which of the members need to be encouraged to participate more in the sharing and discussion times? When and how will I encourage them?

• When could I have responded more appropriately to the needs of members or to the leadership of the Holy Spirit?

• How well did I do at beginning and ending on time?
• Which members most need a visit this week for encouragement, prayer, instruction, correction, or counsel? When will I make the appointment to get together, or when will I "stop by" for the visit?

3. If persons were deeply moved during this session, ask yourself this question about each one: Did the person get all the help he or she needed? If you sense that any need additional help, make plans to provide that help or get the person in touch with someone who can help.

4. Read through "Before the Session" on the following page to get an idea of the preparation that will be required for your next group session.

Session

Love and God's Invitation

Session Goals: This session will help members (1) match three statements about the nature of God with important understandings of how each truth should be applied to the life of a believer; (2) describe the way a person comes to know God personally and intimately; (3) recognize the initiative and activity of God around their own lives; and (4) demonstrate worship of God through prayers and testimonies offered in His name.

AGENDA
1. Arrival Activity (5 Min.)
2. Unit Review (15)
3. Sharing Time (25)
4. Praying Time (10)
5. Singing/Special Music (5)
6. Break (10)
7. Video Viewing and Discussion (45)
8. Closure (5)

BEFORE THE SESSION

❏ Refer to **"Before Every Session"** checklist (LG p. 10) for use with this session.

❏ Gather together the following items and include any others you need for activities that you may have developed on your own.
- one copy of Unit 4 Review Quiz (LG p. 43) and Sharing Time topics (LG p. 43) for each person
- Seven Realities poster
- one copy of Viewing Worksheet 4 (LG p. 44) for each person

❏ Prepare a one-minute preview of Unit 5.

❏ If you are using the videotape, do the following:
- Set up the equipment necessary for viewing.
- Preview the videotape segment for this session and list one or two key ideas or questions that you think will be of special interest to your group. Use these ideas to introduce the videotape.
- Think through your own response to the video discussion question in point 7 of "During the Session" ("Video Viewing and Discussion").
- Prepare to lead youth in a brief discussion using the Viewing Worksheet.

❏ As a review of some important information, read back through LG pages 4-9. Pay special attention to the suggestions for providing spiritual leadership in a group. Continue to review these pages from time-to-time to keep them fresh in your mind.

DURING THE SESSION

1. Arrival Activity

• **Greet members as they arrive**. Give each youth a copy of the unit review quiz to work on while others are coming in. Ask them to be sure they have completed the learning activities that will be discussed in the "Sharing Time."

• **Opening prayer.** Ask members to think of one name by which they have come to know God through experience. Ask each one to pray a sentence prayer of thanksgiving for God's revealing Himself as a personal and living God.

2. Unit Review

• **Review quiz**. Review and discuss, if needed, the answers to the activities on the review quiz. Ask members how they felt when they studied the three truths about God described in the matching activity.

• **Ask volunteers to answer the following questions:**
  a. How do you come to know God personally and intimately? (p. 57)
  b. What are some of the many ways we can worship God through His names? (pp. 58-59)
  c. What is the purpose for God's commands? (p. 62)
  d. How did Jesus know the will of His Father? (p. 12)
  e. What are two factors important to your recognizing God's activity around you? (p. 64)
  f. What are some actions you can take to see if God is at work in a situation? (p. 67)
  g. When does God speak? (pp. 67-68)
  h. When God takes the initiative to accomplish something through an individual or a church, what does He guarantee? (p. 68)

• **Poster discussion**. Focus attention on the statements on the unit posters you have displayed. Read each statement and ask members to comment on what that statement means to them. Ask what adjustments may be needed in their lives to relate correctly to God.

• **Seven realities**. Form pairs. Ask them to state to each other the first three realities of experiencing God.

3. Sharing Time

• **Scripture memory**. Form groups of three or four. Ask them to quote John 14:21 to one another and share what God may have said to them through this week's memory verse. Encourage members to keep up-to-date on their Scripture memorization.

• **Declare the wonderful works of the Lord**. Reassemble the group and allow time for testimonies. Say: If God has done something special in or through your life this last week, please share what God has done so we can praise the Lord together.

• **Focus on God**. Ask: What have you come to know about God, His purposes, or His ways this week? What do you sense God wants you to do in response to this knowledge of Him?

• **Written responses**. Ask youth to turn in their books to the following learning activities and share responses with the person on their right. Topics are listed in the "Sharing Time" box on the review quiz.
  a. An event through which you have come to know God by experience and the name that describes Him (p. 56).
  b. Responses to the following activities:
    i. What you thought, felt, or experienced during your time of worship on Day 2 (p. 59).
    ii. Ideas you may have for recognizing God's activity around you (p. 67).
    iii. One of the most meaningful statements or Scriptures from this unit's lessons and their prayer responses to God. Choose one from pages 57, 62, 65, or 68.

4. Praying Time

• **Share requests and pray.** Using the same groups of three or four formed earlier, ask youth to look at the names of God listed on pages 157-158 and identify one by which they sense a need to know God that way. Then ask them to share with the others the name and why they sense a need to know God that way. For instance, one youth might say, "My parents are divorced, and I have never gotten to know my father. I sense a deep need to know God as a loving heavenly Father." After all youth have shared their sense of need, encourage them to pray specifically for those in their group.

• **Record prayer requests.** As groups finish praying, suggest: Turn to the prayer section of your journal and record prayer requests or ways God led you to pray for individuals in your group.

5. Singing/Special Music

• **Optional special music.** Reassemble the group. Sing a hymn or chorus or play a recorded song that relates to God's names like "His Name Is Wonderful"; "How Majestic Is Your Name"; "Jesus Is the Sweetest Name I Know"; or "We Will Glorify." For special music you might play a recording of "El Shaddai," or another contemporary song.

6. Break

7. Video Viewing and Discussion

• **Introduce the video.** Share one or two key ideas that you think will be of special interest to the youth. Hand out the Viewing Worksheet.

• **View the videotape.** Show the videotape segment for this session.

• **Discussion.** Form groups of three or four. Direct them to discuss the following questions and prepare to share a brief report: Since our church faces so many needs inside and outside our fellowship, how can we do all the many things that need to be done? What are some things we should do?

• **Reporting.** Call for reports and guide a brief discussion as time permits using the Worksheet.

• **Prayer response.** Reassemble the group. Ask two group members to offer prayer responses to God in behalf of your church.

8. Closure

• **Waiting on the Lord.** Review any questions or concerns that may have come up during the session. Ask the group to pray for these concerns and seek answers during the coming week.

• **Preview Unit 5.** Preview Unit 5 by asking members to pay special attention to how God speaks to them in the next two weeks through the Bible and prayer. Suggest they make notes in their journal.

• **Pray.** As members stand together, voice a prayer of praise to God for His great love and a prayer of submission to His will and purposes.

AFTER THE SESSION

---

1. Add to your spiritual journal specific ways you can pray for group members. Do you sense a need to pray intently for any one youth in particular? If so, record concerns you need to pray about for that person.

2. Ask yourself the following questions and jot notes in your spiritual journal or on a separate paper.

• What spiritual or mental preparation do I need to make for the next session that may have been lacking this week?

• Which of the members need to be encouraged to participate more in the sharing and discussion times? When and how will I encourage them?

• When could I have responded more appropriately to the needs of members or to the leadership of the Holy Spirit?

• How well did I do at beginning and ending on time?

• Which member most needs a phone call this week for encouragement, prayer, instruction, correction, or counsel? When will I call?

3. If members have expressed meaningful or inspirational experiences of God's presence, I suggest that you write down a summary of each one. You may also want to ask members to write a one-page summary of their experience of God's presence. These could become a meaningful record of your group experience together. You may have an opportunity to share with other people some of the wonderful works of the Lord. Jot below the names of individuals who shared an inspirational experience of God's activity in his or her life.

4. Read through "Before the Session" on the following page to get an idea of the preparation that will be required for your next group session.

Session

5

God Speaks, Part 1

Session Goals: This session will help members (1) identify three of four important factors in the way God spoke in the Old Testament; (2) state reasons God reveals Himself, His purposes, and His ways; (3) explain how God speaks through the Bible and prayer; and (4) demonstrate concern for a friend by praying for his or her greatest spiritual challenge.

AGENDA

1. Arrival Activity (5 Min.)
2. Unit Review (15)
3. Sharing Time (25)
4. Praying Time (10)
5. Singing/Special Music (5)
6. Break (10)
7. Video Viewing and Discussion (45)
8. Closure (5)

BEFORE THE SESSION

❏ Refer to **"Before Every Session"** checklist (LG p. 10) for use with this session.

❏ Gather together the following items and include items for activities that you may have developed:
  • one copy of Unit 5 Review Quiz and Sharing Time topics (LG p. 37) for each person
  • Seven Realities poster
  • one copy of Viewing Worksheet 5 (LG p. 45) for each person

❏ Prepare two diagrams on poster board. Draw the diagram for the way God speaks through the Bible (p. 81) on one poster and the diagram for prayer (p. 85 on the other. For future *Experiencing God* groups you possibly will want to laminate the posters.

❏ Prepare a one-minute preview of Unit 6. Pay special attention to the activity for preparing a spiritual inventory on page 100, so you can warn members to allow time for it.

❏ If you are using the videotape, do the following:
  • Set up the equipment necessary for viewing.
  • Preview the videotape segment for this session and list one or two key ideas or questions that you think will be of special interest to your group. Use these ideas to introduce the videotape.
  • Think through your own response to the video discussion question in point 7 of "During the Session" ("Video Viewing and Discussion").
  • Prepare to lead youth in a brief discussion using the Viewing Worksheet.

DURING THE SESSION

1. Arrival Activity
  • **Greet members as they arrive**. Give each youth a copy of the unit review quiz to work on while others are coming in. Ask them to be sure they have completed the learning activities that will be discussed in the "Sharing Time."

  • **Opening prayer.** Ask a youth to lead in prayer, thanking God for revealing Himself, His purposes, and His ways.

2. Unit Review
  • **Review quiz**. Review and discuss, if needed, the answers to activities A and C on the review quiz.

  • **Seven realities.** Ask one member to use the Seven Realities poster and review for the group the first four realities of experiencing God.

  • **The Bible and prayer diagrams**. Ask a youth to explain how God speaks through the Bible using the Bible diagram poster. Discuss questions youth may have about the way God speaks through His Word.

  Next ask a different youth to use the prayer diagram poster to explain how God speaks through prayer. Discuss any questions they may have about the way God speaks through prayer.

  • **Poster discussion**. Focus attention on the statements on the unit posters you have displayed. Read each statement and ask youth to comment on what that statement means to them. Ask: What adjustments do you need to make to relate correctly to God?

  • **Ask volunteers to answer the following:**
  a. What is the most important factor we learn from studying the ways God spoke in the Old Testament? (p. 70)
  b. How did God speak in the Gospels? (p. 74)
  c. What is the role of the Holy Spirit in prayer? (pp. 85-86)

3. Sharing Time

• **Written responses**. Form groups of three. Ask youth to turn in their books to the following learning activities and share responses with one another. Topics are listed in the "Sharing Time" box with the review quiz.

   a. What God has been saying in this course (p. 74).
   b. What God has said through the Bible (p. 81).
   c. What God has said through prayer (p. 86).
   d. One of the most meaningful statements or Scriptures from this unit's lessons and your prayer responses to God. Choose one from pages 72, 75, 79, 83, or 87.

• **Focus on God**. Reassemble the group. Ask: What have you come to know about God, His purposes, or His ways this week? What do you sense God wants you to do in response to this knowledge of Him?

• **Declare the wonderful works of the Lord**. Allow time for testimonies. Say: If God has done something special in or through your life this last week, please share what God has done so we can praise the Lord.

• **Scripture memory**. Form pairs. Ask them to quote John 8:47 to each other and share what God may have said to them through this week's memory verse.

4. Praying Time

• **Share requests and pray**. Using the same pairs, ask them to share with each other their greatest spiritual challenge (p. 75). After one member shares the spiritual challenge, ask the partner to pray for him or her. Next, reverse roles and ask the other member to share a spiritual challenge. Then take time for the partner to pray for that person.

• **Record prayer requests**. As pairs finish praying, suggest: Turn to the prayer section of your journal and record the spiritual challenge of your partner, so you can continue to pray for him or her.

5. Singing/Special Music

• **Optional special music**. Reassemble the group. Sing a hymn or chorus or play a recorded song that relates to the Holy Spirit, the Bible, or prayer, such as "Sweet Hour of Prayer"; "Breathe on Me"; "Speak to My Heart"; or "Hark, the Voice of Jesus Calling."

6. Break

7. Video Viewing and Discussion

• **Introduce the video**. Share one or two key ideas that you think will be of special interest to the youth. Hand out the Viewing Worksheet.

• **View the videotape**. Show the videotape segment for this session.

• **Discussion**. Form groups of three or four. Direct them to discuss the following question and prepare to share a brief report: What is the most meaningful thing you learned or reviewed during this message about God's speaking through the Bible and prayer?

• **Reporting**. Call for reports and guide a brief discussion as time permits using the Worksheet.

• **Prayer responses**. Ask a youth to pray in behalf of group members and your church.

8. Closure

• **Waiting on the Lord**. Review any questions or concerns that may have come up during the session. Ask the group to pray for these concerns.

• **Preview Unit 6**. Preview Unit 6 by asking members to pay special attention to the way God may use spiritual markers (Day 4) to guide them in decision making. Tell them to allow time to prepare their own list of spiritual markers before the group session.

• **Pray**. Join hands. Do not suggest a topic for prayer. Rather, suggest that members pray conversationally as the Holy Spirit prompts them.

AFTER THE SESSION

1. Add to your spiritual journal specific ways you can pray for the youth. Do you sense a need to pray for any one person in particular? If so, record concerns you need to pray about for that person. If you heard members mention their greatest spiritual challenges, record them in your prayer list for these members.

2. Ask yourself the following questions and jot notes in your spiritual journal or on a separate paper.

• What spiritual or mental preparation do I need to make for the next session that may have been lacking this week?

• Which of the youth need to be encouraged to participate more in the sharing and discussion times? When and how will I encourage them?

• When could I have responded more appropriately to the needs of members or to the leadership of the Holy Spirit?

• Did I begin and end on time? If not, why?

• Which members most need a letter this week for encouragement? When will I write it?

3. Read through "Before the Session" on the following page to get an idea of the preparation that will be required for your next group session.

Session

6

God Speaks, Part 2

Session Goals: This session will help members (1) write the first four statements of the realities of experiencing God in their own words; (2) identify two possible reasons for silence from God when they pray; (3) explain how to respond when faced with confusing circumstances; and (4) demonstrate an understanding of God's personal guidance in their lives by describing the spiritual markers in their lives.

AGENDA

1. Arrival Activity (5 Min.)
2. Unit Review (15)
3. Sharing Time (25)
4. Praying Time (10)
5. Singing/Special Music (5)
6. Break (10)
7. Video Viewing and Discussion (45)
8. Closure (5)

BEFORE THE SESSION

❏ Refer to **"Before Every Session"** checklist (LG p. 10) for use with this session.
❏ Gather together the following items and include any others you need for activities that you may have developed on your own:
  • one copy of Unit 6 Review Quiz and Sharing Time topics (LG p. 38) for each person
  • Seven Realities poster
  • one copy of Viewing Worksheet 6 (LG p. 45) for each person
❏ Prepare a preview of Unit 7 and be prepared to share the instructions for this preview listed in "During the Session."
❏ If you are using the videotape, do the following:
  • Set up the equipment necessary for viewing.
  • Preview the videotape segment for this session and list one or two key ideas or questions that you think will be of special interest to your group. Use these ideas to introduce the videotape.
  • Think through your own response to the video

discussion question in point 7 of "During the Session" ("Video Viewing and Discussion").
  • Prepare to lead youth in a brief discussion using the Viewing Worksheet.

DURING THE SESSION

1. Arrival Activity
• **Greet members as they arrive**. Give each youth a copy of the unit review quiz to work on while others are coming in. Ask them to follow the instructions in the Sharing Time box for reviewing their list of spiritual markers.
• **Opening prayer.** Lead in prayer and include a request that God speak and work through the members of this group to help others better understand His will for their lives.

2. Unit Review
• **Review quiz**. Review and discuss, if needed, the answers to the questions on the review quiz.
• **Seven realities**. Ask for a volunteer (different from the one who stated the four realities last session) to use the Seven Realities poster and review the first four realities of experiencing God.
• **Ask volunteers to answer the following questions:**
  a. What are two possible reasons for the silence of God when you pray? (p. 91)
  b. What should a Christian do when faced with circumstances that are confusing? (p. 94)
  c. When do you really know the truth of a given situation? (pp. 95-96)
  d. How does a Christian come to understand his or her role in the body of Christ? (pp. 101-103)

3. Sharing Time
• **Spiritual markers**. Share some of your own spiritual markers (assigned on p. 100). Then ask volunteers to share some of the spiritual markers they have identified in their own lives. Ask youth how they sense the use of spiritual markers might help them in decision making. See if someone can give a personal example of how this process is helping them in a specific time of decision right now.
• **Declare the wonderful works of the Lord**. Allow time for testimonies. Say: If God has done something special in or through your life this last week, share

what God has done so we can praise the Lord.

• **Focus on God**. Form groups of three or four. Ask: What have you come to know about God, His purposes, or His ways in relationship to the church? What do you sense God wants our church to do in response to this knowledge of Him?

• **Most meaningful**. Using the groups just formed, ask members to review their five "most meaningful" statements or Scriptures for the unit (pp. 91, 94, 96, 100, or 103) and identify the one statement or Scripture that was most meaningful. Ask members to (a) read their most meaningful statements or Scriptures; (b) tell why they were meaningful; and (c) share how they responded to God in prayer.

• **Scripture memory**. Ask youth to quote John 5:19 to one another in the same groups of three or four and share what God may have said to them through this week's memory verse.

4. Praying Time

• **Share requests.** Reassemble the group. Ask youth to share concerns they have regarding your church or specific members in your church or youth group. Suggest that statements be specific and brief at this point, so the group will have adequate time to pray.

• **Pray.** Again subdivide into groups of three or four, so members can be more actively involved in this prayer time. Ask members to pray specifically for your church and youth group and the members mentioned in the previous sharing time.

• **Record prayer requests**. As groups finish praying ask them to turn to the prayer section of their journals and record their prayer requests.

5. Singing/Special Music

• **Optional special music.** Sing a hymn, chorus, or play a recorded song that relates to God's speaking to and guiding His people. Perhaps a song like "All the Way My Savior Leads Me"; or "He Leadeth Me! O Blessed Thought." Sing special requests or your theme song, as time permits.

6. Break

7. Video Viewing and Discussion

• **Introduce the video.** Share one or two key ideas that you think will be of special interest to the youth. Hand out Viewing Worksheet.

• **View the videotape.** Show the videotape segment for this session.

• **Discussion.** Ask youth to discuss the following questions: What is the most meaningful thing you learned or reviewed during this message about God's speaking through circumstances and the church? How can identifying spiritual markers help you understand clearly what God is doing in your life?

• **Reporting.** Call for reports and guide a brief discussion as time permits using the Worksheet.

8. Closure

• **Waiting on the Lord.** Review any questions or concerns that may have come up during the session. Ask the group to pray for these concerns and seek answers to questions during the coming week.

• **Preview Unit 7.** Preview Unit 7 by asking youth to pay special attention to the four statements listed in "The Crisis of Belief" box on page 107. Ask them to write in the margin of their books any prayer concerns that may come as they study the coming unit. If they have concerns about the way your church or individuals "walk by faith," ask them to pray about those concerns and not discuss them with anyone at this point. Explain that Christa had to surrender her life to God before she could truly walk by faith.

• **Pray.** Join hands in a circle and lead the closing prayer. Ask God to teach all of you this week what walking by faith requires. Ask Him for patience as He guides your whole church to a deeper walk of faith.

AFTER THE SESSION

1. Add to your spiritual journal specific ways you can pray for youth. Do you need to pray intently for any one youth in particular? Record concerns you need to pray about for that youth. Include in your journal any concerns for your church. Pray for these concerns.

2. Ask yourself the following questions and jot notes in your spiritual journal or on a separate paper.

• What spiritual or mental preparation do I need to make for the next session that may have been lacking this week?

• Which of the members need to be encouraged to participate more in the sharing and discussion times? When and how will I encourage them?

• Could I have responded more appropriately to the needs of youth or to the leadership of the Holy Spirit?

• Did I begin and end on time? If not, why?

• Which members most need a call this week for encouragement? When will I call?

3. Read "Before the Session" on the next page for an idea of the preparation required for your next group.

Session

7

The Crisis of Belief

Session Goals: This session will help members (1) state and explain four principles related to the crisis of belief; (2) define faith and identify the opposite of faith; (3) distinguish between actions that indicate faith and those that indicate lack of faith; and (4) demonstrate a willingness to encourage and guide your church to plan for obedience as the body of Christ.

AGENDA

1. Arrival Activity (10 Min.)
2. Unit Review (15)
3. Sharing Time (20)
4. Praying Time (10)
5. Singing/Special Music (5)
6. Break (10)
7. Video Viewing and Discussion (45)
8. Closure (5)

BEFORE THE SESSION

❏ Refer to **"Before Every Session"** checklist (LG p. 10) for use with this session.

❏ Try to help your group pray through any concerns they have about your church. Encourage members to be faithful and respond only to God's leading. His timing will always be right.

❏ Gather the following items and include any others you need for activities that you may have developed on your own:
  • one copy of Unit 7 Review Quiz and Sharing Time topics (LG p. 38) for each person
  • Seven Realities poster
  • one copy of Viewing Worksheet 7 (LG p. 46) for each person

❏ Prepare a one-minute preview of Unit 8 and be prepared to share the instructions for this preview listed in "During the Session."

❏ If you are using the videotape, do the following:
  • Set up the equipment necessary for viewing.
  • Preview the videotape segment for this session and list one or two key ideas or questions that you

think will be of special interest to your group. Use these ideas to introduce the videotape.
  • Think through your own response to the video discussion question in point 7 of "During the Session" ("Video Viewing and Discussion").
  • Prepare to lead youth in a brief discussion using the Viewing Worksheet.

DURING THE SESSION

1. Arrival Activity
  • **Greet members as they arrive**. Give each youth a copy of the unit review quiz to work on while others are coming in. Ask them to be sure they have completed the learning activities that will be discussed in the "Sharing Time."
  • **Opening prayer.** Form groups of three or four. Ask members to share with others in the group a way the group can pray for them. These requests may relate to church, family, personal, or school-related concerns. Encourage members to make the requests brief, so that they will have time to pray. Ask them to pray for the requests mentioned.

2. Unit Review
  • **Seven realities.** Call for a volunteer to explain the fifth reality of experiencing God. Then ask for a volunteer to state at least the first five realities, using the Seven Realities poster.
  • **Review quiz.** Review the four statements under B related to the crisis of belief. For each statement ask members to either state biblical support for the statement or briefly explain what they learned about the particular subject.
  • **Ask volunteers to answer the following questions:**
    a. What is faith and what is an opposite of faith? (p. 108)
    b. Why does God give God-sized assignments that are humanly impossible? (Day 3, pp. 111-113)
    c. What is the relationship between faith and action? (Day 4, pp. 114-117)
    d. According to Hebrews 11, can you determine a person's faith by the good or bad outcome in his life? Why or why not? (p. 119)
  • **Discuss the case study.** Review each of the four case studies on pages 115-116 and ask volunteers to

share their responses to each one. Discuss those on which members have a difference of opinion. Make sure members base their answers on biblical truth and not just human experience. Gently call attention to any effort to base a response on experience alone.

• **Discuss the poster**. Focus attention on the statements on the unit posters you have displayed. Read each statement and ask members to comment on what that statement means to them. Ask what adjustments may be needed in their lives to relate correctly to God.

3. Sharing Time

• **Written responses**. Ask members to turn in their books to the following learning activities and respond as indicated. Topics are listed in the "Sharing Time" box with the review quiz.

   a. Items A-D on page 106. Compare your answers in A and B and discuss responses in C and D.

   c. Times in your life when faith was required and how you responded (p. 110).

   d. Items 1-8 on pages 112-113. Compare your answers to items 1-4. Share, compare, and discuss your responses to items 5-8.

   e. One of the most meaningful statements or Scriptures from this unit's lessons—choose one from pages 107, 110, 113, 117, and 120. Share the statement and your prayer response to God.

• **Declare the wonderful works of the Lord**. Allow time for testimonies. Say: If God has done something special in your life this last week, please share what God has done so we can praise the Lord together.

• **Scripture memory**. Form pairs. Ask them to quote Hebrews 11:6 to each other and share what God may have said to them through this week's memory verse.

• **Focus on God**. Have members discuss these questions in groups of three or four: What have you come to know about God, His purposes, or His ways this week? What do you sense God wants you to do in response to this knowledge of Him?

4. Praying Time

• **Share requests and pray**. Using the same grouping as in the previous activity, ask members to share briefly their concerns about walking by faith as an individual and as a church. Then ask members to pray specifically for one another and for your church.

• **Record prayer requests**. As groups finish praying, suggest: Turn to the prayer section of your journal and record prayer requests or ways God led you to pray for the faith of other believers and for the faith of your church.

5. Singing/Special Music

• **Optional special music**. Reassemble the group.

Sing a hymn or chorus or play a recorded song that relates to faith and action like "Have Faith in God" or "Faith Is the Victory." For special music you might consider playing a recording of "Find Us Faithful."

6. Break

7. Video Viewing and Discussion

• **Introduce the video**. Share one or two key ideas that you think will be of special interest to the youth. Hand out the Viewing Worksheet.

• **View the videotape**. Show the videotape segment for this session.

• **Discussion**. Ask members to discuss the following questions and prepare to share a brief report: What did Henry mean by "planned disobedience"? What are some ways you sense our church or youth group needs to commit itself to planned obedience? (Response to this second question might include a commitment to reach every person in your community for Christ and respond whenever God shows you where He is at work. It could include a commitment related to church planting or mission projects.)

• **Reporting**. Call for reports and guide a brief discussion as time permits using the Worksheet.

• **Prayer response**. Ask one group member to offer a prayer response in behalf of your church.

8. Closure

• **Waiting on the Lord**. Review any questions or concerns that may have come up during the session. Ask the group to pray for these concerns and seek answers to questions during the coming week.

• **Preview Unit 8**. Preview Unit 8 by asking members to pay special attention to the kinds of adjustments that may be required for a person to move into the mainstream of God's activity.

• **Pray**. Ask members to join hands in a circle and pray for your church and for one another as you regularly face the crisis of belief.

AFTER THE SESSION

1. Add to your spiritual journal specific ways you can pray for group members. Do you sense a need to pray intently for any one person in particular? If so, record concerns you need to pray about for that person. Include in your spiritual journal any concerns for your church that may have surfaced during the session. Pray for these concerns during the coming week.

2. Ask yourself the following questions and jot notes in your spiritual journal or on a separate paper.

- What spiritual or mental preparation do I need to make for the next session that may have been lacking this week?

- Which of the members need to be encouraged to participate more in the sharing and discussion times? When and how will I encourage them?

- When could I have responded more appropriately to the needs of members or to the leadership of the Holy Spirit?

- How well did I do at beginning and ending on time?

- Which member most needs a visit or call this week for encouragement, prayer, instruction, correction, or counsel? When will I visit or call?

3. Read through "Before the Session" below to get an idea of the preparation that will be required for your next group session.

Session
8

Adjusting Your Life to God

Session Goals: This session will help group members to (1) state six of the seven realities of experiencing God; (2) determine ways a person waits upon the Lord; (3) identify ways God has led them to make adjustments in their own lives; and (4) demonstrate a commitment to the lordship of Christ by verbalizing a prayer of surrender.

AGENDA

1. Arrival Activity (5 Min.)
2. Unit Review (15)
3. Sharing Time (25)
4. Praying Time (10)
5. Singing/Special Music (5)
6. Break (10)
7. Video Viewing and Discussion (45)
8. Closure (5)

BEFORE THE SESSION

❑ Refer to **"Before Every Session"** checklist (LG p. 10) for use with this session.
❑ Gather together the following items and include any others you need for activities that you may have developed on your own:
  - one copy of Unit 8 Review Quiz and Sharing Time topics (LG p. 39) for each person

- Seven Realities poster
- chalkboard and chalk or newsprint and a marker
- (optional) a copy of *The Notebook: A DiscipleYouth Experience* to show members how this course may be of help in training and developing prayer ministries in the local church (refer to session 3, "Talking to God")
- one copy of Viewing Worksheet 8 (LG p. 46) for each person
❑ If you are using the videotape, do the following:
  - Set up the equipment necessary for viewing.
  - Preview the videotape segment for this session and list one or two key ideas or questions that you think will be of special interest to your group. Use these ideas to introduce the videotape.
  - Think through your own response to the video discussion question in point 7 of "During the Session" ("Video Viewing and Discussion").
  - Prepare to lead youth in a brief discussion using the Viewing Worksheet.

DURING THE SESSION

1. Arrival Activity
- **Greet members as they arrive.** Give each youth a copy of the unit review quiz to work on while others are coming in. Ask them to be sure they have completed the learning activities that will be discussed in the "Sharing Time."

- **Opening prayer.** Call on a member to pray, asking God to guide all group members to make the adjustments that He desires of them.

2. Unit Review

• **Review seven realities**. Display your Seven Realities poster. Point to the arrow at the top and ask a member to state the first reality. Turn to the next person in the circle and ask her to state the second reality. Continue around the circle until you have stated at least the first six realities. Mention that, in the next unit, members will be studying the seventh reality in detail.

• **Review quiz**. Review and discuss, if needed, the answers to the questions on the review quiz for Unit 8 (p. 13). Spend time discussing members' written responses to the two questions in part C. Ask, What does a person do while he is "waiting on the Lord"? As group members respond, write their responses on a chalkboard or newsprint. (Answers: pray, watch circumstances, share with and listen to other believers, continue doing the last thing God told you to do—pp. 136-137)

• **Ask volunteers to answer the following questions:**

   a. What is required as a demonstration of faith? (p. 122)

   b. Who are some of the people in the Bible who had to make adjustments to God? What adjustment did each one have to make? (p. 122)

   c. Who is one Bible character that was asked to make an adjustment but refused? (p. 123)

   d. What are some kinds of adjustments that you may have to make in order to obey God? (p. 125)

   e. Does God ever ask a person to change his or her own plans and directions in order to follow God's purposes? (p. 129) Do you think God will ever ask you to change your plans and directions in order to follow Him? (Note: If some answer no to this second question, remind them that they cannot stay where they are and go with God. God will always require an adjustment in order to follow Him.)

• **Poster discussion**. Focus attention on the statements on the unit posters that you have displayed. Read each statement and ask members to comment on what that statement means to them. Ask what adjustments may be needed in their lives to relate correctly to God.

3. Sharing Time

• **Scripture memory**. Form pairs. Ask them to quote Luke 14:33 to each other and share what God may have said to them through this week's memory verse.

• **Written responses**. Form groups of three or four. Ask them to turn in their books to the following learning activities and share responses with one another. Topics are listed in the "Sharing Time" box with the review quiz.

   a. One of the most meaningful statements or Scriptures from this unit's lessons and your prayer response to God. Choose one from pages 124, 127, 130, 134, and 138.

   b. Adjustments you have made in your thinking during this course (p. 126).

   c. Major adjustment(s) God has required of you (p. 126).

   d. An experience in which costly adjustment or obedience was required (p. 130).

   e. The quotation on pages 126-127 that was most meaningful and why.

   f. How your church and youth group would be seen in regard to prayer and adjustments that God may want them to make (p. 138).

• **Declare the wonderful works of the Lord.** Reassemble the group. Allow time for testimonies. Say: If God has done something special in or through your life this past week, please share what God has done so we can praise the Lord together.

• **Focus on God**. Ask: What have you come to know about God, His purposes, or His ways this week? What do you sense God wants you to do in response to this knowledge of Him?

4. Praying Time

• **Sharing and recording prayer requests**. Ask members to turn to the prayer request section of their spiritual journals. Ask them to share specific requests that they have about their own prayer lives and the prayer life in your church.

• **Pray.** In the groups of three or four formed earlier, have members pray conversationally for the requests just mentioned.

• **Prayer life**. If some in your group have a deep burden about the prayer life of your church, suggest that they refer to the "Talking to God" section in *The Notebook: A DiscipleYouth Experience*. This section gives special attention to the prayer life of believers.

5. Singing/Special Music

• **Optional special music.** Sing a hymn or chorus or play a recorded song that relates to submission to God's will or making adjustments like "I Surrender All"; "All to Thee"; or "He Is Lord."

6. Break

7. Video Viewing and Discussion

• **Introduce the video.** Share one or two key ideas that you think will be of special interest to the youth. Hand out Viewing Worksheet.

• **View the videotape.** Show the videotape segment for this session.

• **Discussion.** Ask members to discuss the following

questions and prepare to share a brief report: What examples or reasons would you give to defend the statement: "It may be more costly not to adjust than to adjust?" What does this statement mean: "Don't hold in your heart what you can hold in your hand"?

• **Reporting.** Call for reports and guide a brief discussion as time permits using the Worksheet.

• **Prayer response.** Ask one youth to offer a prayer response in behalf of individuals and your church.

8. Closure

• **Waiting on the Lord.** Review any questions or concerns that may have come up during the session. Ask the group to pray for these concerns and seek answers to questions during the coming week.

• **Preview Unit 9.** Preview Unit 9 by sharing that the focus of the next unit is on obedience. Some of your members will find this to be a very difficult study as they evaluate their own level of obedience. You will need to give them a word of encouragement. Read Matthew 28:18-20. Point out that one of the church's assignments is to help her members *obey*. Mention that, in the next session, members will be able to help, encourage, and pray for one another in the area of obedience.

• **Pray.** Ask members to join hands in groups of three and pray about adjustments they may need to make in response to God. Encourage members to give absolute surrender to Christ's lordship and to pray for one another as well. Tell them they are dismissed as they finish praying in their groups. Remind them to be quiet while others finish praying.

AFTER THE SESSION

1. Add to your spiritual journal specific ways you can pray for group members. Do you sense a need to pray intently for any one person in particular? If so, record concerns you need to pray about for that person.

2. Ask yourself the following questions and jot notes in your spiritual journal or on a separate paper.

• What spiritual or mental preparation do I need to make for the next session that may have been lacking this week?

• Which of the members need to be encouraged to participate more in the sharing and discussion times? When and how will I encourage them?

• When could I have responded more appropriately to the needs of members or to the leadership of the Holy Spirit?

• How well did I do at beginning and ending on time?

• Which member most needs a note this week for encouragement? When will I write and mail the note?

3. Read through "Before the Session" for session 9 to get an idea of the preparation that will be required for your next group session.

Session

9 *Experiencing God Through Obedience*

Session Goals: This session will help members (1) state in order all seven of the realities of experiencing God; (2) identify the importance and meaning of obedience; (3) explain why Christian maturity often is a slow process; (4) demonstrate their worship of God by sharing ways they have personally experienced God; and (5) demonstrate their commitment to strengthen one another by praying for the spiritual growth and maturity of each member.

AGENDA

1. Arrival Activity (5 Min.)
2. Unit Review (15)
3. Sharing Time (20)
4. Praying Time (10)
5. Singing/Special Music (5)
6. Break (10)
7. Video Viewing and Discussion (45)
8. Closure (10)

BEFORE THE SESSION

❑ Refer to **"Before Every Session"** checklist (LG p. 10) for use with this session.

❑ Gather together the following items and include any others you need for activities that you may have developed on your own:
- one copy of Unit 9 Review Quiz and Sharing Time topics (LG p. 39) for each person
- Seven Realities poster
- chalkboard and chalk or newsprint and a marker
- one copy of Viewing Worksheet 9 (LG p. 47) for each person

❑ Contact the church office or the appropriate person and check the church calendar for possible dates for a fellowship to celebrate the completion of the course. You could have the fellowship soon after the completion of the study, or you could wait until you have received the *Experiencing God, Youth Edition,* diplomas, so they can be given out at the fellowship. If you choose this second option, set a date four to six weeks away to provide time to order and receive the diplomas. Whatever choice you make, plan to invite other youth in your church.

❑ If you are using the videotape, do the following:
- Set up the equipment necessary for viewing.
- Preview the videotape segment for this session and list one or two key ideas or questions that you think will be of special interest to your group. Use these ideas to introduce the videotape.
- Think through your own response to the video discussion question in point 7 of "During the Session" ("Video Viewing and Discussion").
- Prepare to lead youth in a brief discussion using the Viewing Worksheet.

DURING THE SESSION

1. Arrival Activity
• **Greet members as they arrive**. Give each youth a copy of the unit review quiz to work on while others are coming in. Ask them to be sure they have completed the learning activities that will be discussed in the "Sharing Time."

• **Opening prayer**. Paraphrase Psalm 119:33-35 (p. 143) to become a group prayer by using us, we, and our, instead of I, me, and my. Ask group members to voice their agreement with this prayer by praying in unison: We love You, Lord, so we will obey You.

2. Unit Review
• **Seven realities**. Form pairs. Ask them to state to each other the seven realities in order. Display the Seven Realities poster, in case a person needs the diagram as a prompt.

• **God's pattern**. After the pairs finish, reassemble the group. Remind the group that the realities are not steps or a method to follow. Rather, the seven statements describe God's pattern of working with His people. He always takes the initiative—we do not take the initiative in accomplishing God's purposes. Say: We have studied these seven realities of God so that you will be able to identify God's activity in your life. Now, when God takes the initiative to involve you in His work, I trust that you will know how to respond to Him by acting in faith, making the necessary adjustments, and obeying Him.

• **Ask volunteers to answer the following questions:**
   a. How important is obedience? (pp. 141-142)
   b. What is the meaning of obedience? (p. 144)
   c. When a person disobeys God, does God give that person a second chance? Explain your answer. (pp. 145-146)
   d. Why does God sometimes work slowly in a person's life to bring the person to maturity? (p. 152)
   e. What are some of the things you would do when faced with a circumstance that seemed to close the door on God's will? (p. 153) (Write responses to this question on a chalkboard or newsprint.)

• **Poster discussion**. Focus attention on the statements on the unit posters. Read each statement and ask members to comment on what that statement means to them. Ask what adjustments may be needed in their lives to relate correctly to God.

3. Sharing Time
• **Scripture memory**. Form pairs. Ask members to quote John 14:23 to each other and share what God may have said to them through this week's memory verse.

• **Written responses**. Using the same pairs, ask members to turn in their books to the following learning activities and share responses with each other. Topics are listed in the "Sharing Time" box with the review quiz.
   a. Statements that have influenced the way you love and obey God (p. 141).
   b. Names by which you have come to know God through experience (p. 151).
   c. Items A-G on pages 144-145.
   d. Statements that have been meaningful to you (p. 148).
   e. Items B through G on page 155.
   f. Items H and I on pages 155-156 and why you responded as you did.
   g. One of the most meaningful statements or

Scriptures from this unit's lessons and your prayer response to God. Choose one from pages 143, 147, or 150.

• **Focus on God**. Ask: What have you come to know about God, His purposes, or His ways this week? What do you sense God wants you to do in response to this knowledge of Him?

• **Declare the wonderful works of the Lord**. Allow time for testimonies. Say: If God has done something special in your life this last week, please share what God has done so we can praise the Lord together.

4. Prayer Time

• **Share requests and pray**. In pairs, ask members to share with their partners one area of obedience that they presently struggle with or one act of obedience that they know God is guiding them to do. Then ask members to pray for their partners and their specific need in the area of obedience.

Form groups of three or four. Ask members to turn to page 156 and share responses to items J and K. After one person shares, ask the other members of the group to stand around the person and pray for his or her request. Continue until all youth have been prayed for.

• **Record prayer requests**. As groups finish praying, suggest: Turn to the prayer section of your journal and record prayer requests or ways God led you to pray for other members.

5. Singing/Special Music

• **Optional special music**. Sing a hymn or chorus or play a recorded song that relates to obedience or experiencing God at work. Use songs like "Living for Jesus" or "Make Me a Channel of Blessing."

6. Break

• **Provide refreshments**. Provide some kind of light refreshments and spend a few extra minutes informally celebrating the fellowship and study you have shared during the past 10 weeks. Encourage members to get refills just prior to the video viewing.

7. Video Viewing and Discussion

• **Introduce the video**. Introduce the videotape by sharing one or two key ideas that you think will be of special interest to the members. Hand out the Video Viewing Worksheet 9.

• **View the videotape**. Show the videotape segment for this session.

• **Discussion**. Ask members to discuss the following questions and prepare to share a brief report: What is the relationship between obedience and character? How is character related to an assignment God may have for you?

• **Reporting**. Call for reports and guide a brief discussion as time permits using the Worksheet.

• **Prayer response**. Ask one group member to offer a prayer response in behalf of individuals, your youth group, and your church.

8. Closure

• **Set a date.** Guide members in selecting a date for the after-study get-together. Let the group decide whether to have the fellowship soon after the completion of the study or after the diplomas arrive.

• **Pray.** Stand in a circle and join hands. Close with a period of thanksgiving to God for all the wonderful things He has done during this study. Ask members to pray about one "thanksgiving" at a time, but encourage them to pray as many times as they want.

AFTER THE SESSION

1. Add to your spiritual journal a final list of specific ways you want to continue praying for group members, other members of your youth group, and for your church.

2. Have members complete the "Church Study Course Enrollment/Credit Request" form (p. 160, LG p. 48). Make sure all the information is correct and complete. Sign and date the forms and mail them to: Church Study Course Awards Office, Baptist Sunday School Board, 127 Ninth Avenue, North, Nashville, TN 37234. Diplomas normally will be returned in four weeks.

3. Involve group members in planning and preparing for the after-study fellowship. Send out invitations or call members to remind them of the date and time.

4. Take some time, perhaps on a half-day retreat, to evaluate your group-study of *Experiencing God, Youth Edition*. Use the following questions to start your thinking. Make notes for yourself on a separate sheet of paper or in your journal. Begin this time of evaluation with a period of prayer for God's perspective.

• How has God used this study to influence or improve your relationship with Him?

• What has God done in the life of your church or youth group as a result of this study?

• What do you think was the most meaningful experience of the study?

• What would you do differently in a future study of the course? (Consider things such as enlistment of participants, size of group, meeting time and place, learning activities, prayer times, and others.)

• What should you do next? Lead another group?

Study or teach another DiscipleLife course? Begin or facilitate a new ministry?

5. Encourage youth to complete the *"Experiencing God, Youth Edition,* Course Evaluation'' (LG p. 40). Review their responses. Make summary notes on the things you think you would change with the next small group you lead through this study.

6. Store the following materials for use with future small-group studies of *Experiencing God, Youth Edition.*
   • Memorizing Scripture poster
   • Seven Realities poster

• unit posters from Units 1-9
• *Experiencing God Youth Video Series*
• notes you have written that are not included in this Leader's Guide
• other materials you have prepared for the group sessions

7. Spend time in prayer and fellowship with God, thanking Him for all He has done in your life and church during the past 10 weeks.

Scriptures for Meditation

The following Scriptures relate to subjects in *Experiencing God, Youth Edition.* They may be meaningful to you during and after your study of *Experiencing God.* Mark these in your Bible, study them, meditate on them, and even memorize some of them. These verses are from the *New International Version* of the Bible.

Numbers 14:35	Isaiah 31:1	John 3:16	2 Corinthians 5:19
Deuteronomy 4:7	Isaiah 40:31	John 6:44	Galatians 2:20
Deuteronomy 4:29	Isaiah 41:10	John 6:63	Galatians 5:6
Deuteronomy 6:4-5	Isaiah 46:11	John 6:65	Ephesians 3:20-21
Deuteronomy 11:26-28	Isaiah 48:17	John 7:17	Philippians 1:6
Deuteronomy 30:19-20	Isaiah 55:8-9	John 8:31-32	Philippians 2:13
2 Chronicles 16:9	Isaiah 64:4	John 8:36	Philippians 3:8
Psalm 5:3	Jeremiah 17:5-7	John 10:10	Philippians 3:10
Psalm 25:4-5	Jeremiah 31:3	John 12:26	Philippians 4:13
Psalm 33:11	Jeremiah 33:3	John 14:6	Philippians 4:19
Psalm 37:4-5	Daniel 3:17	John 14:26	Colossians 2:8
Psalm 37:7	Amos 3:7	John 15:10	Colossians 2:9-10
Psalm 40:8	Zechariah 4:6	John 15:16	Colossians 3:4
Psalm 42:1	Matthew 6: 31-33	John 16:8	Hebrews 1:1-2
Psalm 63:1	Matthew 7:21-23	John 16:13	Hebrews 11:1
Psalm 86:11	Matthew 10:24-25	John 17:3	Hebrews 13:8
Psalm 126:5-6	Matthew 10:39	Acts 1:8	James 1:3-4
Psalm 127:1	Matthew 25:21	Romans 8:26-27	James 1:5
Proverbs 3:5-6	Mark 9:23	Romans 8:28	James 2:26
Isaiah 1:18-20	Luke 6:46	Romans 8:35, 37	James 4:8
Isaiah 14:24	Luke 9:23-24	1 Corinthians 2:9	1 John 3:16
Isaiah 26:12	Luke 10:22	1 Corinthians 15:10	1 John 4:9-10
Isaiah 30:1	Luke 11:28	1 Corinthians 4:2	1 Peter 4:10

Keeping a Spiritual Journal

Throughout this course you will have experiences in your spiritual life that you will want to record for later reference. When God speaks to you, you will want to write down what He has said. You also will be given opportunities to pray specifically for members of your group and for your church. You will need a notebook of some kind.

Assignments in the notebook will fall into four large categories. You may choose to create other categories if you want to.

1. Testimonies. This section is for diary accounts of what God is doing in, around, and through your life and what you have learned about Him, His purposes, and His ways.

2. Daily Review. At the end of each day's work, you will be asked to review the lesson and identify the most meaningful statement or Scripture and then respond to God. The daily review section of your journal provides extra space for you to record summaries of what God is saying to you through His Word, prayer, circumstances, and the church. It also can include summaries of adjustments you sense God wants you to make, directions you sense God is calling you to follow, steps of obedience called for, and other responses God may be calling you to make to Him.

3. Weekly Review. Use the questions in the "Spiritual Journal Weekly Review" box at the right to review what God has done during the past week.

4. Prayer Requests. This section will be used in each group session for recording prayer requests and answers to prayer for individuals and for your church. It can be divided to include requests such as:

- Personal requests
- Requests for group members
- Requests for my church
- Other special requests

SPIRITUAL JOURNAL WEEKLY REVIEW

Keeping a spiritual journal will help you remember the important things God says to you and the things He does in your life. Use the following questions to review God's activity in your life each week during this course of study. You only need to respond to those questions that apply to what God has done or revealed.

1. What has God revealed to you about Himself?

2. What has God revealed to you about His purposes?

3. What has God revealed to you about His ways? (How He acts, what He does, how He responds in given circumstances, the kind of people He uses, the ways He involves people in His work, the ways He goes about accomplishing His purposes)

4. What has God done in your life or through your life that has caused you to experience His presence?

5. What Scripture has God used to speak to you about Himself, His purposes, or His ways?

6. What particular person or concern has God given you a burden to pray for? What has He guided you to pray regarding this person or concern?

7. What has God done through circumstances that has given you a sense of His timing or direction concerning any aspect of His will?

8. What word of guidance or truth do you sense that God has spoken to you through another believer?

9. What adjustment is God leading you to make in your life?

10. What acts of obedience have you taken this week? What acts of obedience do you know God is wanting you to take?

Experiencing God—Unit 1

John 15:5

"I am the vine; you are the branches. If a man remains in me and I in him, he will bear much fruit; apart from me you can do nothing."

—**John 15:5, NIV**

Experiencing God—Unit 2

Psalm 20:7

Some trust in chariots and some in horses, but we trust in the name of the LORD our God.

—**Psalm 20:7, NIV**

Experiencing God—Unit 3

Matthew 22:37-38

Jesus replied: "'Love the Lord your God with all your heart and with all your soul and with all your mind.' This is the first and greatest commandment."

—**Matthew 22:37-38, NIV**

Experiencing God—Unit 4

John 14:21

"Whoever has my commands and obeys them, he is the one who loves me. He who loves me will be loved by my Father, and I too will love him and show myself to him."

—**John 14:21, NIV**

Experiencing God—Unit 5

John 8:47

"He who belongs to God hears what God says. The reason you do not hear is that you do not belong to God."

—**John 8:47, NIV**

Experiencing God—Unit 6

John 5:19

Jesus gave them this answer: "I tell you the truth, the Son can do nothing by himself; he can do only what he sees his Father doing, because whatever the Father does the Son also does."

—**John 5:19, NIV**

Experiencing God—Unit 7

Hebrews 11:6

Without faith it is impossible to please God, because anyone who comes to him must believe that he exists and that he rewards those who earnestly seek him.

—**Hebrews 11:6, NIV**

Experiencing God—Unit 8

Luke 14:33

"Any of you who does not give up everything he has cannot be my disciple."

—**Luke 14:33, NIV**

Experiencing God—Unit 9

John 14:23

Jesus replied, "If anyone loves me, he will obey my teaching. My Father will love him, and we will come to him and make our home with him."

—**John 14:23, NIV**

You have permission to reproduce this page for use with your Experiencing God group.

UNIT 1 REVIEW QUIZ

Write a key word or words for each of the seven realities of experiencing God.

1. _____

2. _____

3. _____

4. _____

5. _____

6. _____

7. _____

Check your answers using the inside back cover of your book.

Get Acquainted

A. My name is . . .

B. The thing I like best about my hometown is . . .

C. I accepted Jesus Christ as my Lord and Savior when . . .

D. Something interesting you might not know about me is . . .

E. I chose to study this course on knowing and doing the will of God because . . .

- -

UNIT 2 REVIEW QUIZ

A. Mark the following statements as T (true) or F (false).

____ 1. God asks people to dream up what they want to do for Him (p. 26).

____ 2. God always takes the initiative in my relationship to Him (p. 30).

____ 3. I know God's will by following a correct formula (p. 35).

____ 4. The moment God speaks is God's timing (p. 36).

B. Use the words below to complete the following statements.

      ability   belief   character   unbelief

1. Asking God for a sign is an indication of _____ (p. 35).

2. God develops _____ to match the assignment (p. 37).

Check your answers using the pages cited in parentheses.

Sharing Time—Unit 2

- The statements about God's judgment in the section "You Need to Know What God Is About to Do" (p. 28).

- The four questions on lordship and character building at the bottom of page 37.

- One of the most meaningful statements or Scriptures from this unit's lessons and your prayer response to God. Choose one from pages 26, 29, 32, 35, or 38.

- -

UNIT 3 REVIEW QUIZ

A. Which of the following ought to be the primary influence in shaping your life? (pp. 43-44)
❑ My past
❑ My future

B. Who takes the initiative ("first step") in establishing a love relationship between you and God? (p. 48)
❑ I do
❑ My pastor does
❑ God does

C. Fill in the blanks to complete the second reality of experiencing God. (inside back cover)

God _____ a continuing _____

that is _____ and _____ .

Check your answers using the pages cited in parentheses.

Sharing Time—Unit 3

- Things in which you are investing your life, time, and resources and the adjustments God wants you to make (p. 45).

- Reasons you know God loves you (p. 48).

- An experience when God was real, personal, or practical in His relationship to you (p. 52).

- One of the most meaningful statements or Scriptures from this unit's lessons and your prayer response to God. Choose one from pages 42, 45, 50, or 53.

UNIT 4 REVIEW QUIZ

A. Match the fact about the nature of God on the left with the correct statement of application on the right. Write the correct letters in the blanks (p. 61).

_____ 1. God is love.
_____ 2. God is all-knowing.
_____ 3. God is all-powerful.

A. God's directions are right.
B. God can enable me to do His will.
C. God's will is best.

B. Fill in the blanks in the third reality of experiencing God (p. 63).

God invites you to become _____ with Him in His _____.

C. List at least three things only God can do (pp. 66-67).

_____

_____

_____

Check your answers using the pages cited in parentheses.

Sharing Time—Unit 4

- An event through which you have come to know God by experience and the name that describes Him (p. 56).
- (Move to groups of four.) What you thought, felt, or experienced during your time of worship on Day 2 (p. 59).
- Ideas you may have for recognizing God's activity around you (p. 67).
- One of the most meaningful statements or Scriptures from this unit's lessons and your prayer response to God. Choose one from pages 57, 62, 65, or 68.

- -

UNIT 5 REVIEW QUIZ

A. Using the hints below, write the other three important factors in the way God spoke to individuals in the Old Testament (pp. 70-71).

1. When God spoke, it was usually unique to that individual.

2. Sure _____

3. What _____

4. Encounter _____

B. When God speaks by the Holy Spirit, what are three things He reveals? (p. 78)

God speaks by the Holy Spirit to reveal: _____,
His _____, and His _____.

C. Match the things God reveals with the correct reason. Write the correct letters in the blanks (p. 79).

God reveals . . .

_____ 1. Himself

_____ 2. His purposes

_____ 3. His ways

Because . . .

A. He wants me to know how to accomplish things only He can do.
B. He wants me to know what He is about to do so I can join Him.
C. He wants me to have faith to believe He can do what He says.

Check your answers using the pages cited in parentheses.

Sharing Time—Unit 5

- What God has been saying in this course (p. 74).
- What God has said through the Bible (p. 81).
- What God has said through prayer (p. 86).
- One of the most meaningful statements or Scriptures from this unit's lessons and your prayer response to God. Choose one from pages 72, 75, 79, 83, or 87.

UNIT 6 REVIEW QUIZ

Using the hints below, write the first four statements of the realities of experiencing God in your own words (inside back cover).

1. Work _____

2. Relationship _____

_____

3. Invitation _____

4. Speaks _____

_____

_____

Check your answers on the inside back cover.

Sharing Time—Unit 6

• Spiritual markers in your own life (assigned on p. 100).

- - - - - - - - - - - -- - - - - - - - - - -- - - - - - - - - - - -- - - - - - - - - - - - - - - - -- - -- - - - - - - - - - -

UNIT 7 REVIEW QUIZ

A. In your own words, write a statement of the fifth reality of experiencing God using the hint below (inside back cover).

Crisis _____

_____

B. Fill in the blanks in the following four statements (p. 118).

1. An encounter with God requires _____

2. Encounters with God are God- _____

3. What I do in response to God's _____

   (invitation) reveals what I _____ about God.

4. True faith requires _____.

Check your answers using the page cited in parentheses.

Sharing Time—Unit 7

• Items A-D on page 106. Compare your answers in A and B and discuss your responses in C and D.

• Times in your life where faith was required and how you responded (p. 110).

• Items 1-8 on pages 112-113. Compare your answers to items 1-4. Share, compare, and discuss your responses to items 5-8.

• One of the most meaningful statements or Scriptures from this unit's lessons. Choose one from pages 107, 110, 113, 117 or 120. Share the statement and your prayer response to God.

UNIT 8 REVIEW QUIZ

A. Fill in the blanks to complete the statements we have been studying in this unit (p. 135).

1. You cannot _____ where you are

    and _____ with God at the same time.

2. Obedience is _____ to _____

    and to those around you.

3. Obedience requires _____ _____

    on God to work through you.

B. Which of the following is the best way to find God's directions for your life or your church. Check only one.
   ❏ a. A good book
   ❏ b. Other people
   ❏ c. God
   ❏ d. Denominational agency

C. On the back of this sheet answer the following:

1. Why must you depend totally on God to work through you to accomplish Kingdom purposes? (p. 135)
2. Why should you "wait on the Lord"? (p. 136)

Check your answers using the pages cited in parentheses.

Sharing Time—Unit 8

• One of the most meaningful statements or Scriptures from this unit's lessons and your prayer response to God. Choose one from pages 124, 127, 130, 134, or 138.
• Adjustments you have made in your thinking during this course (p. 126).
• Major adjustment(s) God has required of you (p. 126).
• An experience where costly adjustment or obedience was required (p. 130).
• The quotation that was most meaningful and why (pp. 126-127).
• How your church and youth group would be seen in regard to prayer and adjustments God may want your church or youth group to make (p. 138).

- -

UNIT 9 REVIEW QUIZ

Now you have studied all seven of the realities of experiencing God. Using the hints below, write the seven statements in your own words.

1. God's work _____

2. Love relationship _____

3. God invites _____

_____

4. God speaks _____

_____

5. Crisis of belief _____

6. Major adjustments _____

_____

7. Obey Him _____

_____

Check your answers using the inside back cover of your book.

Sharing Time—Unit 9

• Statements that have influenced the way you love and obey God (p. 141).
• Names by which you have come to know God through experience (p. 151).
• Items A-G on pages 144-145.
• Statements that have been meaningful to you (p. 148).
• Items B through G on page 155.
• Items H and I on pages 155-156 and why you responded as you did.
• One of the most meaningful statements or Scriptures from this unit's lessons and your prayer response to God. Choose one from pages 143, 147, or 150.

EXPERIENCING GOD, YOUTH EDITION, COURSE EVALUATION

Group Leader:_____ Date: _____

Your responses to the following are intended to help your group leader grow in his or her ability to guide the group sessions of future studies of *Experiencing God, Youth Edition.* Complete this form prayerfully.

1. What did you like most about your group leader?

2. What would you suggest your group leader could do with future groups that would make learning and the group experience even better?

3. What kinds of activities were most meaningful to you during the group sessions? Why?

4. What kinds of activities were least meaningful to you? Why?

5. If you could choose only one thing, what would you want to spend more time doing during the group sessions? Why?

6. What, if anything, would you suggest spending less time on during the group sessions? Why?

7. How would you sum up what this study has done to help you in your walk with the Lord?

8. What do you sense God has revealed during this study that He wants to do in and through your life in the days ahead? (Be specific.)

9. What major adjustments do you sense God is leading you to make in order to join Him in His work?

10. During this study, what was your most meaningful experience of God's work or activity in or through your life? Explain what God did.

11. Write a prayer to God for what He has done in your life during this study.

Worksheet 2: Seven Realities of Experiencing God

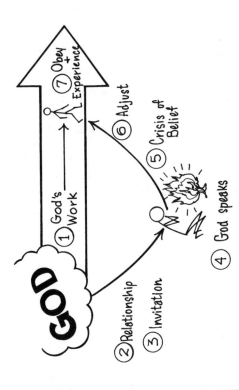

1. God is always at work around you.

2. God pursues a continuing love relationship with you that is real and personal.

3. God invites you to become involved with Him in His work.

4. God speaks by the Holy Spirit through the Bible, prayer, circumstances, and the church to reveal Himself, His purposes, and His ways.

5. God's invitation for you to work with Him always leads you to a crisis of belief that requires faith and action.

6. You must make major adjustments in your life to join God in what He is doing.

7. You come to know God by experience as you obey Him, and He accomplishes His work through you.

Worksheet 1: Jesus' Example

"My Father is always at his work to this very day, and I, too, am working.

"I tell you the truth, the Son can do nothing by himself; he can do only what he sees his Father doing, because whatever the Father does the Son also does. For the Father loves the Son and shows him all he does. Yes, to your amazement he will show him even greater things than these."

—John 5:17, 19-20, NIV

Read John 5:17, 19-20 and answer the following questions.

1. Who is always at work? _____

2. How much can the Son do by Himself? _____

3. What does the Son do? _____

4. Why does the Father show the Son what He is doing? _____

The verses you just read contain the clearest statements of how Jesus knew what to do. I would outline Jesus' approach to knowing and doing God's will like this:

Jesus' Example

- The Father has been working right up until now.
- Now God has Me working.
- I do nothing on My own initiative.
- I watch to see what the Father is doing.
- I do what I see the Father already is doing.
- You see, the Father loves Me.
- He shows Me everything that He, Himself, is doing.

Video Viewing Worksheet for Leader Preparation

As you view this *VHS Tape 1 for Leaders,* look for the points below and complete this Worksheet. Use additional paper if necessary. Understanding these points will help you in your preparation. Familiarize yourself with the concepts and ideas in the Leader's Guide. Work through the entire study before leading a small-group. Spend time in prayer.

"I think that probably the greatest tragedy in our churches today is that we are under-challenging the teenagers. . . . I think many of them will turn around later and say, 'You betrayed me. All you did was entertain me. But you didn't challenge me.' I have never seen any age group that responds more deeply and with greater sacrifice and a deeper kind of commitment than teenagers."—Henry Blackaby

♦ God has always worked with youth. ♦ Youth today respond with incredible commitment. ♦ They are waiting for someone to give them a challenge that matches what they feel in their heart. ♦ This may be the last generation that God calls. The Lord may return in our lifetime.

GOD USES. . . A Person of Absolute Integrity and A Person with a Solid and Healthy Family Life
      1. How is your prayer life?
      2. How is your witness?
      3. Are you guilty of creating a "credibility gap"?

PERSONAL AND SPIRITUAL GOALS
♦ To meet God. You can cover the material in 13 weeks but you can't meet God in 13 weeks.
♦ To present every teenager perfect in Christ *(Col. 1:28-29).* God's goal is to conform us to the image of His Son *(Rom. 8:29).*
    Keep a spiritual journal. Use it to keep up with the spiritual growth of your youth. After the first session record the characteristics you see present in the lives of your youth. Following the completion of Unit 4 take an inventory to see how they are growing.

SMALL-GROUP CONSIDERATIONS
- Size of Group
- Age and Gender
- When to Meet
- Where to Meet

ENLISTING YOUTH TO JOIN THE BIBLE STUDY
❑ Don't do it all on your own.
❑ Don't worry about numbers. Begin with one, if necessary.
❑ Ask God to show you which youth have a heart for Bible study.
❑ Trust God to do the multiplication.
❑ Don't say, "Nobody wants to come." The one that comes is SOMEBODY.
❑ Embrace the miracle of the loaves and fish.
❑ Develop the "long look."

❑ Make a long-term commitment to your youth.
❑ Pray that God will begin His work with you and the other adults in your church.
❑ Don't tell God how He is to begin the process of bringing the teenagers from not wanting to study the Bible to studying the Bible. Ask Him to show you where He wants to begin.
❑ CAUTION: There is nothing more deadening than having a person lead a Bible study that even you would not want to attend.

THE IMPORTANCE OF BEING A ROLE MODEL
♦ Jesus modeled what He taught. ♦ Communication is more than verbalizing. ♦ Character communicates.

1. Where do you see God at work in your personal life, family life, church, work, lives of your youth?

2. Dr. Blackaby states that "The reason many of us can't convince teenagers that God is at work is because we don't know the Scriptures well enough." How familiar are you with God's Word?

3. What is one thing that you hope to learn personally through your involvement in leading youth through *Experiencing God?*

4. Read John 6:44. What does this verse say about our responsibility in reaching others?

5. What does Philippians 2:13 tell us about our motivation and ability to do God's will?

Jot Notes Here While Viewing

Video Viewing Worksheet 1

Listen for the following truths. Check off some truths you find interesting. Add other truths to this list that you find interesting. Make a note of any question or comment you have.

"God is big enough to create the universe, but He's also personal enough to be your dad."

"No one can come to me unless the Father who sent me draws him" (John 6:44a, NIV).

God will always reveal where He is at work.

Principles for Recognizing God's Activity in Your Life

- ❑ Get to know God well enough so you will know when He is alerting you.
- ❑ Don't just sit and wait for God to bring a revelation.
- ❑ Waiting takes on a new meaning: shifting the responsibility of the outcome to God.
- ❑ Do the last thing God told you to do.

Discuss After Viewing the Video

- ◆ What adjustments do you need to make to God in your personal life, in your school relationships, in your family, or in your church relationships?
- ◆ Why is it important to make your decisions based on biblical principles?
- ◆ Why can't you stay the way you are and go with God?

Video Viewing Worksheet 2

Listen for the following truths. Check off some truths you find interesting. Add other truths to this list that you find interesting. Make a note in the margin or on the back of this worksheet of any question or comment you have.

"God gives you the opportunity and it's your choice to follow Him."

God wants you to know where He is at work. Adjust your mind and heart so you will see Him.

No temptation has seized you except what is common to man. And God is faithful; he will not let you be tempted beyond what you can bear. But when you are tempted, he will also provide a way out so that you can stand up under it (1 Cor. 10:13, NIV).

> *"Do not worry about tomorrow, for tomorrow will worry about itself. Each day has enough trouble of its own" (Matt. 6:34, NIV).*

Chosen by God:
- ❑ *"Before I formed you in the womb I knew you"* (Jer. 1:5a, NIV).
- ❑ God had chosen Paul before he was born. He just chose to announce it on the road to Damascus *(Acts 9)*.
- ❑ *For he chose us in him before the creation of the world (Eph. 1: 4a, NIV).*

Discuss After Viewing the Video

- ◆ How have you been guilty of telling God what you want to do for Him, rather than waiting on God to give you instructions?
- ◆ Using a specific example, explain how you have limited God's right to interrupt your life.
- ◆ Are open and closed doors always indications of God's directions? Why or why not?

Video Viewing Worksheet 3

Listen for the following truths. Check off some truths you find interesting. Add other truths to this list that you find interesting. Make a note of any question or comment you have.

"God cares so much about you. It's not something that we pursue or we initiate. God initiates it totally."

According to *Romans 3* nobody seeks after God. What if God didn't seek after you?

As important as a daily quiet time is, it's not enough to experience God. Jesus always spent time with the Father, but the real encounter with God came when He came out of that time into the real world.

God did not create us for time but for eternity. Time is the opportunity to come to know, love, and obey God.

Our experience with God does not depend on what we have experienced.

Your Life Is the Product of the Choices You Make.

- ➤ The relationship God wants to have with you will be real, personal, and practical.
- ➤ God takes the initiative, He chooses you, loves you, and reveals His eternal purposes for your life.
- ➤ I have my quiet time because I know God and love Him, not in order to learn about Him.

Discuss After Viewing the Video

- ◆ Can a person actually have a real, personal, and practical relationship with God?
- ◆ How much time and effort are you investing in a personal, intimate relationship with God?
- ◆ Discuss specific examples of how God can guide you to invest your life in worthwhile ways.

Video Viewing Worksheet 4

Listen for the following truths. Check off some truths you find interesting. Add other truths to this list that you find interesting. Make a note in the margin or on the back of this worksheet of any question or comment you have.

"The reason God put us on earth is to be with Him."

- ❏ The desire will be consistent with the nature of Christ.
- ❏ If it is selfish, the Spirit of God will convict you through His Word.
- ❏ If you're not in the Scripture, you better worry.

For it is God who works in you to will and to act according to his good purpose (Phil 2:13, NIV).

Accepting the Assignment:
- ❏ God's assignments match your character.
- ❏ God is going to develop your character.
- ❏ God never mismatches character and assignment.

You may want to be great. But if you have a small character God won't give you a big task.

God's love has never changed. The cross doesn't change because things get bad. Don't let any circumstance convince you that God doesn't love you.

Discuss After Viewing the Video

- ◆ What is the difference between knowing about God and knowing God?
- ◆ How does knowing God's nature (love, all-powerful, all-knowing) affect your worship? your attitude? your actions?
- ◆ In your experience with God have you found His commandments to be restricting or freeing?

Video Viewing Worksheet 5

Listen for the following truths. Check off some truths you find interesting. Add other truths to this list that you find interesting. Make a note of any question or comment you have.

"The way I hear God most is in my quiet time when I'm wanting to hear what He says."

Sometimes you can't hear God speak because you clutter your life with worldly things.

There is room for your desires and opinions in God's work as long as their source is from God.

If Talking About God Speaking to You Doesn't Seem Natural:
❑ You may not be talking about God much. So. . . talk about how God spoke to you in your youth group.
❑ You may need to use other terms. Like. . . God is real to me and He's given me some direction. While I was praying I really sensed God leading me.
❑ Regularly talk about God working in your life—it could be a great conversation starter.

Discuss After Viewing the Video

◆ What does the following statement mean: "When I come to the Word of God, the Author Himself is present to instruct me"?
◆ How do you know when God is speaking to you?
◆ How does knowing God strengthen your faith to do His work?

Video Viewing Worksheet 6

Listen for the following truths. Check off some truths you find interesting. Add other truths to this list that you find interesting. Make a note in the margin or on the back of this worksheet of any question or comment you have.

"I hear God speak through circumstances—by the people I meet and the opportunities I have to share God with other people."

❑ Silence might mean that you have gotten sidetracked and you don't recognize God's voice like you used to.
❑ If you are no longer sensing that God is speaking the problem is probably you.
❑ There are some times when God allows you to seek Him.
❑ Silence drives you back to God. He catches your attention.
❑ Silence is not a negative. It's not rejection. It's God's alert system to keep you focused.

"I am the good shepherd; I know my sheep and my sheep know me" (John 10:14, NIV).

You should expect to hear from God just as you would expect to hear from a friend. We have made God speaking to us so extraordinary that we don't expect to hear from Him.

In a moment of crisis we call on God. He's been here all the time. Recognizing this could have prevented the time from being as bad as it was for us.

If hearing and obeying God involves a group decision and someone feels led in a different direction, someone is not hearing God correctly. In group life like the church the spirit of God gives one heart and one mind. An individual call will likely be unique.

Discuss After Viewing the Video

◆ When a circumstance is confusing, what are some steps you can take to understand the circumstance?
◆ How can the idea of identifying spiritual markers help you understand more clearly what God is doing in your life?

Video Viewing Worksheet 7

Listen for the following truths. Check off some truths you find interesting. Add other truths to this list that you find interesting. Make a note of any question or comment you have.

"I believe God stretches us to our limits because He wants true followers. He doesn't want people who sit on the fence."

The "crisis of belief" is that moment when God speaks. Whatever you do next reveals what you believe about God.

When God calls you to join Him in a God-sized assignment He usually wants to develop your character. God wants you to know Him better than ever before. Are you always looking for the comfort zone?

God will let you know what your assignment is. It will be unique. Don't look for a burning bush.

Discuss After Viewing the Video

◆ Discuss the statement, "What you do tells what you believe."

◆ What is meant by the statement, "Faith without action is dead"?

◆ What impact can you have in your world when you allow God to use you in a God-sized assignment?

Jot Notes Here While Viewing

Jot Notes Here While Viewing

Video Viewing Worksheet 8

Listen for the following truths. Check off some truths you find interesting. Add other truths to this list that you find interesting. Make a note of any question or comment you have.

"I'm ready to have God interrupt my life. I'm going to have to change the way I do things."

If you are personally ready to make an adjustment in your life but your family and friends aren't:

❑ Take time to see why they are responding the way they are.
❑ If they're not Christians give them time to adjust with you to your lifestyle in Christ.

The length of the waiting time depends on what God is asking you to do.
- You can share your faith now, but
- A call to attend college must come later (after high school).

Discuss After Viewing the Video

◆ What examples or reasons would you give to defend the statement: "It may be more costly not to adjust than to adjust"?

◆ "Obedience requires total dependence on God to work through me." What is meant by "total dependence"?

Video Viewing Worksheet 9

Listen for the following truths. Check off some truths you find interesting. Add other truths to this list that you find interesting. Make a note of any question or comment you have.

"Obedience is the major key in disciplining yourself. You have the choice to live your life the way you want or live your life the way God wants you to … Obedience is the major thing."

It is costly not to obey God. But God does give second chances.
The moment you repent God…
- picks you up,
- forgives you,
- and gives you an assignment that will be far more significant than if you had not responded at the second chance He gave you.

You will know when you have completed what God has asked you to do by the peace that God will give you.

Discuss After Viewing the Video

◆ Do you always receive affirmation for your obedience to God? At what point do you receive affirmation?
◆ Do you believe God gives second chances? Defend your answer with specific examples.
◆ How has God used this study to influence or improve your relationship with Him?

Resource Ordering Information

Orders or order inquiries may be sent to Customer Service Center, 127 Ninth Avenue, North, Nashville, TN 37234, or call 1-800-458-2772. Telephone representatives are available between 8:00 a.m. and 5:30 p.m. Central Time, Monday—Friday. In Canada, call 615-251-2643, collect. West Coast customers call 1-800-677-7797. The printed materials also are available at Baptist Book Stores and LifeWay Christian Book Stores nationwide.

- *Experiencing God: Knowing and Doing the Will of God, Youth Edition* (Item 7200-08) for members
- *Experiencing God Leader's Guide, Youth Edition* (Item 7200-07) for leaders
- *Experiencing God Youth Video Series* (Item 7700-48)
- *Lift High the Torch: An Invitation to Experiencing God* (Item 7200-51)
- *DiscipleHelps: A Daily Quiet Time Guide and Journal* (Item 7217-45)
- *DiscipleNow Manual* (Item 7255-78)
- Spanish—*Experiencing God, Youth Edition* (Item 7200-47)
- Spanish—*Experiencing God, Youth Edition, Leader's Guide* (Item 7200-48)

The Church Study Course

The Church Study Course is a Southern Baptist education system designed to support the training efforts of local churches. It provides courses, recognition, record keeping, and regular reports for some 20,000 churches.

This education system is characterized by short courses ranging from 2 1/2 to 10 hours in length. They may be studied individually or in groups. With more than 600 courses in 24 subject areas, it offers 130 diploma plans in all areas of church leadership and Christian growth. Complete details about the Church Study Course system, courses available, and diplomas offered may be found in a current copy of the *Church Study Course Catalog*. The Church Study Course system is jointly sponsored by many agencies within the Southern Baptist Convention.

An *Experiencing God, Youth Edition*, diploma is awarded for completion of this study. The courses are:

Course 1: 03-388—Units 1-2—Experiencing God–Youth: God's Will
Course 2: 03-389—Units 3-4—Experiencing God–Youth: Love Relationship
Course 3: 03-390—Units 5-6—Experiencing God–Youth: God Speaks
Course 4: 03-391—Unit 7—Experiencing God–Youth: Crisis of Belief
Course 5: 03-392—Unit 8—Experiencing God–Youth: Major Adjustments
Course 6: 03-393—Unit 9—Experiencing God–Youth: Obedience

How to Request Credit for This Course

This book is the text for course numbers 03-388, 03-389, 03-390, 03-391, 03-392, 03-393, in the subject area: Christian Growth and Service. The course is designed for 9 hours of group study. Credit for these courses may be obtained through a combination of individual and group study. Read the entire book and complete the learning activities as you read. Attend a group study session for each unit. If you are unable to attend one or more group sessions, make arrangements with the group leader to complete and make-up work that he or she assigns.

A request for credit may be made on Form 725 and sent to the Awards Office, Sunday School Board, 127 Ninth Avenue, North, Nashville, TN 37234. The form below may be used to request credit. Enrollment in a diploma plan may also be made on Form 725.

Within three months of your completion of a course, confirmation of your credit will be sent to your church. A copy of your complete transcript will be sent to your church annually during the July-September quarter, if you have completed a course during the previous 12 months.

Duplicate Form Below As Needed

CHURCH STUDY COURSE
ENROLLMENT/CREDIT REQUEST
FORM - 725 (Rev.1/93)

MAIL THIS
REQUEST TO ▶

CHURCH STUDY COURSE RESOURCES SECTION
BAPTIST SUNDAY SCHOOL BOARD
127 NINTH AVENUE, NORTH
NASHVILLE, TENNESSEE 37234

Is this the first course taken since 1983? ☐ **YES** If yes, or not sure complete all of Section 1. ☐ **No** If no, complete only bold boxes in Section 1.

SECTION 1 - STUDENT I.D.	SECTION 3 - COURSE CREDIT REQUEST

STUDENT

Social Security Number | Personal CSC Number*

☐ Mr ☐ Miss ☐ Mrs. DATE OF BIRTH ▶ Month Day Year

Name (First, MI, Last)

Street, Route, or P.O.Box

City, State | Zip Code

CHURCH

Church Name

Mailing Address

City, State | Zip Code

SECTION 3 - COURSE CREDIT REQUEST

Course No.	Title (Use exact title)
1. 03-388	Experiencing God-Youth: God's Will (Units 1-2)
2. 03-389	Experiencing God-Youth: Love Relationship (Units 3-4)
3. 03-390	Experiencing God-Youth: God Speaks (Units 5-6)
4. 03-391	Experiencing God-Youth: Crisis of Belief (Unit 7)
5. 03-392	Experiencing God Youth: Major Adjustments (Unit 8)
6. 03-393	Experiencing God-Youth: Obedience (Unit 9)

SECTION 4 - DIPLOMA/CERTIFICATE ENROLLMENT

Enter exact diploma/certificate title from current Church Study Course catalog. Indicate age group/or area if appropriate. Do not enroll again with each course. When all requirements have been met, the diploma/certificate will be mailed to your church. Enrollment in Christian Development Diplomas is automatic. No charge will be made for enrollment or diplomas/certificates.

SECTION 2 CHANGE REQUEST ONLY (Current Inf. in Section 1

☐ Former Name

☐ Former Address | Zip Code

☐ Former Church | Zip Code

Title of Diploma/Certificate	Age group or area
Experiencing God, Youth Edition, Diploma	
Title of Diploma/Certificate	Age group or area
Signature of Pastor, Teacher, or Other Church Leader	Date

*CSC # not required for new students. Others please give CSC # when using SS # for the first time. Then, only one ID # is required. SS# and date of birth requested but not required.